not on fiche

LC65-15733

D0513923

THE INQUISITION

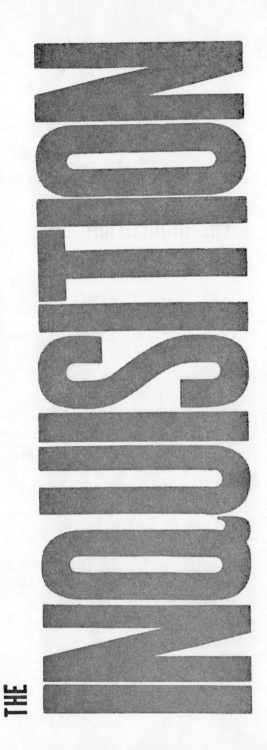

THE INQUISITION

Fernand Hayward

Translated by: Malachy Carroll

Original title: **Que Faut-il Penser de l'Inquisition?**
Published by Librairie Arthème Fayard, Paris.

Nihil Obstat: John A. Goodwine, J.C.D., Censor Librorum
Imprimatur: Terence J. Cooke, D.D., V.G.
New York, N.Y.—June 11, 1965

The Nihil Obstat and Imprimatur are official declarations that a book or pamphlet is free of doctrinal or moral error. No implication is contained therein that those who have granted the nihil obstat and imprimatur agree with the contents, opinions or statements expressed.

Library of Congress Catalog Card Number: 65-15733

Designed, printed and bound in the U.S.A. by the Pauline Fathers and Brothers of the Society of St. Paul as a part of their Communications Apostolate.

"In order to understand - not to justify - the judgments and practices of the Church in the past, we must take into account the historical and social conditions of those times of intolerance."

Bernard Haring, "The Liberty of the Children of God," ALBA HOUSE, Staten Island, New York, 1966

Contents

Part One

THE EPISCOPAL INQUISITION AND THE ROMAN INQUISITION

CHAPTER ONE

Has the Church the Right to Coerce?

The reader will bear with us if we begin somewhat unexpectedly with a quotation from the *Syllabus*. In Proposition XXIV of this celebrated document, the complement to the Encyclical *Quanta cura*, published in 1864, Pius IX solemnly condemns the following error: *Ecclesia vis inferendae potestatem non habet*: "The Church has not the right to use force."

The *Syllabus*, in effect, is a catalogue of highly diverse propositions, ranging from undoubted heresy to assertions which are more or less dangerous and more or less debatable in foundation or form. The meaning of *vis* in Proposition XXIV provides matter for discussion. Does it refer simply to the power of spiritual coercion (excommunication, interdict) or to the power of temporal coercion, extending even to the death penalty? It is agreed this proposition does assert the Church's incontestable right to spiritual coercion. No competent theologian would now assert the Church's right to coerce physically.

We have begun with this text because it contains in brief the problem of a right exercised by the Church, a right by which, in different countries and in a variety of ways, the Court of the Inquisition was established and conducted.

Undoubtedly, the word *Inquisition* casts a shadow of repulsion. It causes a shudder among those whose knowledge of this famous Court has been obtained only from the French Encyclopedists and from the Romantics.

Everyone knows that chapter in Voltaire's *Candide* headed: "How a splendid *auto da fe* was held to prevent the earthquakes"... and what follows. Candide and Doctor Pangloss are each dressed in a San-Benito, crowned with a mitre, and led in procession to the place where the ceremony is to be held. A Biscayan and two Portuguese, convicted of having refused to eat bacon, are burned alive, Candide is flogged and Doctor Pangloss is hung. Of course, Doctor Pangloss will escape. All this has been decided on by the Doctors of Coimbra to prevent an earthquake, but the earthquake occurs that very day. This is all very amusing, but it gives a very inexact impression of the Inquisition, even considered in its most somber aspect.

Unfortunately, it is not easy to escape the irony of Voltaire. The image he has created of the Inquisition, especially that of Spain and Portugal, is really a ludicrous caricature, but so brilliantly done that it has left an impression by no means easy to eradicate.

However unpleasant certain facts concerning the Inquisition may be, and however painful to certain present-day Catholics, the Inquisition is none the less a matter of history which it is as well to study, especially as it confronts us with a problem which can be met only with complete frankness.

First of all, it is important to consider the principle by virtue of which the Church, having received her mission to lead souls to salvation by teaching them revealed truths and the rule of life derived from those truths, must protect the deposit of Faith. To deny this truth would be to deny the very authority of the Church and the solid foundations of Catholicism.

Saint Paul was the first to implement this principle of spiritual coercion inherent in the nature itself of the Church. In his First Epistle to Timothy (1, 18-20), he writes: "This charge, then, I give into thy hands, my son Timothy, remembering how prophecy singled thee out long ago. Serve, as I bade thee, in this honorable warfare, with faith and a good conscience to aid thee. Some, though refusing this duty, have made shipwreck of their faith; among them, Hymenaeus and Alexander, whom I have made over to Satan, till they are cured of their blasphemies." Again, writing to Titus, Saint Paul says: "Give a heretic one warning, then a second, and after that avoid his company; his is a perverse nature, thou mayest be sure, and his fault has been admitted on his own confession" (3, 11 — Msgr. Knox's translation).

These two texts from Saint Paul justify the punishment of excommunication and of interdict. If the Church has the right to guard her children from error, she has equally the right to lead back those who have gone astray: for, by the very fact of their Baptism, heretics are subject *volentes nolentes* (willy-nilly) to the laws of the Church they seek to deny.

It is a complete falsifying of perspectives to maintain, as some have done, that Christians, who complained bitterly of being victims of odious intolerance in the time of persecution, were themselves transformed into odiously intolerant persecutors as soon as full liberty was assured to them after Constantine. Here, for instance, in Rafael Sabatini, biographer of Torquemada: "From the very moment when the new religion found itself recognized and endowed, not only with civil rights, but with effective power; from the very moment when the Christians could move about openly and without fear, we see them consecrating themselves to persecutions directed against those of another cult, against Jews, pagans and heretics. Indeed, although Christianity was only in the fourth century of its existence, not only had it powerfully and irresistibly developed in spite of the efforts to repress it, but also it was already beginning to experience divisions within itself. It has been calculated that, in the fourth century, the number of schisms was no less than ninety."

There is here a confusion, conscious or unconscious, which falsifies the import of the whole matter. It is sufficient to enumerate the heresies which proliferated during the first Christian centuries, to realize that the Church would have failed in her mission if she had not severely condemned them and had not done all in her power to preserve her children from contamination by them. Urged by Quodvuldeus, deacon of Carthage, the aged Saint Augustine wrote the first part of a work on the heresies, a work which his death prevented him from completing. The natural mildness of Augustine did not prevent him from manifesting extreme severity towards those who, often with cunning, pretense and dissimulation, propagated false doctrines.

Nevertheless, we must distinguish between the relentless and tenacious war waged by the Church against error and the propagation of error, on the one hand, and, on the other, the question of resort to force and to constraint in order to achieve her aims.

This resort implies the close union of religious power and civil power—in other words, it implies that the state is to assist the Church by taking preventive measures against those who, in a Christian society, prove to be disturbers of public order because of the trouble they cause in religious matters. In effect, from the time when through Baptism the ruler became a son of the Church, every injury to the integrity and purity of the faith constituted a crime of treason against the Divine, which society through its duly invested representatives, had the right and the duty to punish. This was the thinking of the times. One finds the fourth century Pope, Anastasius I, and the fifth century Popes, Saint Innocent I, Saint Leo the Great, Saint Hormisdas, Saint Gregory the Great, not only combatting heresy with the utmost energy, but handing over to the civil authority—to "the secular arm," as it would later be described—those, who, having been apprehended and admonished, continued obstinate in their error. Nor was this confined to the Popes; the Councils, often assembled for the purpose of examining, judging and condemning a heresy, would formally appeal to the imperial authority to intervene and to prevent the heretics from exercising their influence.

The Councils of Aquileia (381), of Milan (389) at which Saint Ambrose presided, of Carthage (404), of Milevum (416), of Orleans (538), of Toledo (589), made such an appeal to the civil authority.

In those primitive times, we are clearly far removed from the period when a special tribunal would be set up to inquire—*inquirere,* whence "Inquisition"—into the purity of the Faith, and consequently into the erroneous doctrines threatening its integrity. But the vigilance exercised by the bishops and the Councils, and even directly by the Popes themselves, already raises the question of the nature and limits of the Church's coercive power. It was, until recently, a highly controversial issue, where opposite opinions were held among Catholic authorities, to say nothing of others. However, some constant factors can be discerned more or less clearly in this tangle of interpretations, inductions and deductions, especially the frequently enunciated principle that the Church abhors the shedding of blood—*Ecclesia horret a sanguine.*

Dealing with the punishments to be inflicted on heretics, Saint Augustine excludes all recourse to violence. He suggests only spiritual penalties and moral constraints, but he does admit, in certain cases, the use of the rod—a punishment which is not cruel and which, he somewhat amusingly recalls, is that inflicted by schoolmasters on their pupils.

This attitude of the Church towards violent punishment and especially towards the death sentence was an absolutely genuine one; she would even place under interdict a bishop who, through excessive zeal, had compelled the secular authority to pronounce sentence of death. This occurred, for instance, in connection with the fourth century Spanish heretic Priscillian. When Priscillian, Bishop of Avila, was first condemned by the Council of Saragossa (380), he went to Rome to argue his case with Pope Saint Damasus. Refused a hearing by this Pope and then by Saint Ambrose, he had to appear again before a council assembled at Bordeaux. Rather than be judged by his peers, Priscillian appealed to the Emperor Maximus, who summoned him before his court together with his accusers, Bishops Ithacius of Sossuba and Idacius of Emerita. Saint Martin of Tours tried to persuade Ithacius to drop the charge lest Priscillian should be condemned to death, and while he remained in Treves, where the Emperor resided, he was successful in preventing this. However, when Saint Martin left Treves, Maximus, at the instigation of the bishops, handed over the accused to the prefect, Evodius. Priscillian was convicted of heresy, magic and evil practices, and, together with six of his followers, was burned alive (385). This sentence was received with general reprobation among the clergy; and Ithacius, even in Spain where Priscillian had been condemned with great severity, found that his fellow bishops would have nothing to do with him. Despite his repentance, he was deposed.

This example—one of many that could be cited— is sufficient to show the extent to which the Church of that time had a predominantly spiritual and wholly maternal idea of her coercive power.

If we are to appreciate the difference between the period we have just been discussing and the later period in which the Court of the Inquisition was officially instituted, one essential point must not be overlooked.

While the Western Empire still existed, society was
not entirely Christian. No doubt, the post-Constantine
Church enjoyed full freedom and had the support of
the public powers. But traces of paganism remained
and, generally speaking, although they had multiplied
very considerably, the Christians at that period were
somewhat of an elite.

In the fourth and fifth centuries, and even later,
we are far from that theocratic conception of the
world which Saint Thomas defined in his *Summa*, and,
following him, Dante in his *De Monarchia*, and upon
which the *Divine Comedy* is entirely based. Though
she was fully conscious of her coercive power and of
her duty to combat error energetically in all its forms,
the Church at that earlier period adopted a defensive
rather than an offensive attitude. The reason for this
was that she was still at the stage when she had yet to
transform and remodel the ancient pagan society in
the midst of which she was born, and which developed,
she would ultimately dominate. By the twelfth century—
the century in which the Inquisition was established—
that same society had been entirely Christianized.
Whereas Saint Augustine, in his *City of God*, had to
fight against a declining paganism, the medieval Doctors
and Popes—Gregory VII or Innocent III, for instance—
were concerned with strongly establishing the principle
of papal supremacy even over the civil power. When
disruptive elements arose to disturb this pre-established
harmony, it was for the ecclesiastical authority and the
civil authority to collaborate in eliminating such a
cause of disorder.

CHAPTER TWO

The Albigenses and the Waldenses

The current term "the age of Faith," applied in particular to the twelfth and thirteenth centuries, suggests a misleading image of the late Middle Ages. It was, of course, the great age of cathedrals, which gradually spread throughout France, England, Germany, Italy and Spain; it was the age when outstanding monuments of Christian thought, such as the works of Saint Bernard and the *Summa* of Saint Thomas, proclaimed the triumph of Catholicism. But what conflicts were the price of that triumph! Before condemning the Inquisition as something totally evil, it is as well to consider, at least in broad outline, those strange doctrines and those more or less open or secret movements whose gradual extension threatened the very foundations of society itself, and not merely the foundations of the Christian religion.

One aspect must be emphasized first and foremost,

when we speak about the sect of the *Cathari*, the most dangerous of all the heretical bodies of the time, and about the havoc it caused especially in Southern France. It was not only the anti-social character of the Albigensian heresy which determined the intervention of Saint Dominic, the thunders of Innocent III, the Crusade of Simon de Montfort, and the explicit institution of the Court of the Inquisition by Gregory IX; it was, above all, the fact that, in the Middle Ages, all propagation of heretical doctrine of any kind, was looked upon, not only as a crime against the established Church, but also as a crime against society, whose structure was modeled on the same Church.

This being understood, it remains that Catharism or Albigensianism, even more than the heresy of the Waldenses, wrought social havoc over a long period in the places to which it spread. Catharism, whose adherents multiplied in the West, especially from the twelfth century, was to a large extent a re-emergence of third century Manicheism. Mani (216-276), called by the Greeks Manes and by the Latins Manichaeus, had attempted an impossible synthesis of Christian doctrine, Oriental ideas, and Greek philosophy. Plato, Pythagoras, Zoroaster, Iranian Mazdeism, Buddhism, all contributed to this curious mixture.

That a Principle of Good and a Principle of Evil presided at the Creation is the fundamental dualism which characterizes both Manicheism and Catharism. From the Principle of Good emanate the spiritual nature and the New Law revealed by Christ: this is the principle of light. From the Principle of Evil, the principle of darkness, proceed corporeal beings and the Law of Moses. According to this doctrine of dualism, man has two souls. One soul is intellectual and endowed with reason; the other is an evil soul from which the body derives its life and which is the source of all sin. The Manicheans held that Christ assumed only a phantom body, a body in appearance only. Since souls are coeternal with God, Baptism with water they regarded as useless, and they also denied the existence of free will. Mani, the author of these theories, was born a slave in Asia Minor. His mistress, a widow, not only freed but also adopted him. He devoted himself to learned and subtle speculations, and assumed the character of a wonder-worker, a pretension which ruined him. Having promised to raise to life the dead child of King Sapor, he failed in the attempt and was burned alive by royal command. Manicheism spread through the entire East, penetrated even into China, and had also considerable success in the West. Nevertheless, the sect met with a powerful adversary in the person of one of its former adherents, Saint Augustine, who fought against it with great energy and eloquence.

It might be supposed that, in the twelfth century, Manicheism would have been just remote history, and yet there it was, emerging in a new form in the West. About 1140, it was noticed that a strange sect was beginning to infiltrate into the Rhinelands and the Netherlands. The clergy of Liege, denounced this sect to Pope Lucius III, and Saint Bernard, alerted by the provost of Steilfeld, began to combat it with his customary vigor. It was something profoundly evil. The members of the sect held doctrines stemming directly from Manicheism, with additional elements borrowed from Gnosticism and from Donatism. Realizing that Southern France was also infected by this heresy, Saint Bernard went there in 1145 and found a worse state of affairs in Languedoc and in Gascogne than existed in the North.

The sect whom the Abbot of Clairvaux set out to combat was none other than that of the Cathari. Strictly speaking, it was not new; as we have seen, its roots stretched back through eight centuries. Although opposed and persecuted, the Manicheans had continued to flourish in the Byzantine Empire, greatly assisted in this by the constant troubles there. From Constantinople, where they were known as Bogomiles, they passed into the Balkans, Rumania, Bosnia, Dalmatia. From there they reached Italy, and they are known to have had seven churches in Lombardy in the twelfth century. Gradually the sect extended into Tuscany and to Viterbo, Spoleto, and Orvieto. It was in the face of a situation of such obvious gravity that Pope Innocent III decided to undertake the war against the Cathari. However, on account of the incessant clashes between Guelfs and Ghibellines, in consequence of the controversy on investitures, conditions in Northern Italy and even in Rome were such that the Pope preferred Languedoc as the first field of action. There was also the fact that the situation there was more serious than in Lombardy.

It is hard to determine whether southern France was contaminated from Italy or whether the heresy was implanted there by students and merchants coming straight from the East. The latter supposition would explain the name *Bougres*—a corruption of the word *Bulgar*—then used in France for the Cathari. At all events, the heresy spread simultaneously in northern and southern France, though its success and its influence were far more extensive in the southern provinces.

The Cathari were far from having a doctrine absolutely coherent and accepted by all. Their ideas about the creation of the world varied from group to group. According to the Monarchians, the Good God created the original chaos and divided it into four elements; then the Evil God, Satan-Lucibel, seized upon these to create the world. According to the dualists, Satan-Lucibel had not the power to create the world *ex nihilo*. (The reader who wishes to pursue this further must be referred to an excellent work by Belperron: *La Croisade des Albigeois*.) God having created the world, Lucibel decided to populate it. He managed to get into heaven, and there he seduced to his cause a number of angels. Having lured them on to the earth, he gave them a body and formed Adam and Eve from the ooze of the sea; then he caused them to increase and multiply. At each birth, Satan draws on his reserve of fallen angels to fit a soul to a new body. Thus, for the Christian idea of original sin the Cathari substituted another notion, that man is guilty because he has fled from heaven. Moved by compassion, the Good God called together the faithful angels and asked for a volunteer who would descend on earth and bring to men the revelation by which they could be set free. Jesus volunteered, and thus became the Son of God. But since, as an emanation of the Good God, Jesus could have no contact with matter, his body was a body in appearance only. The immediate conclusion from these premises was that the God of the Old Testament is the Bad God, his servants being the patriarchs, Moses and the prophets, while the doctrines of the Incarnation and the Redemption became meaningless. It was Satan who, by means of the Jewish people, determined and secured the passion and crucifixion of Christ; but both the passion and crucifixion were in appearance only since, not having a real body, Jesus could neither suffer nor die.

All this was a mass of cloudy fantasies, in which one again finds a curious hodge-podge of Manicheism, Gnosticism and Docetism. The Church, having the sacred charge of souls, could not permit the faithful to be contaminated by such gross errors, especially as those errors proved able to seduce, not only the simple and the unlettered, but even men of high intelligence and education. For instance, in the south of France, certain ecclesiastical dignitaries and religious communities joined the sect.

For that reason alone, therefore, the Church was bound to intervene. But the evil was not limited to this perversion of minds, for Catharism, by its very doctrine, tended to nothing less than the destruction of the human race. It therefore constituted a social danger of the highest order.

The Cathari rejected the sacraments, including Baptism, and replaced them by a single rite, *the consolamentum*, by virtue of which the recipient was filled with the Holy Spirit—that Spirit, however, not being for these heretics the Third Person of the Blessed Trinity. They alone who had received *the consolamentum* could be saved. If a person received it on his deathbed, his soul would enter into heaven and would take its place among the faithful angels. If such a person recovered, however, he was to avoid coming again under the power of matter, under pain of undergoing the fate of the "non-consoled," destined to a series of purifying re-incarnations. The reception of *the consolamentum*, to which every member was to aspire, would make him one of the "perfect," the sect being composed of "the Perfect" and "the Believers." Since in the Catharist doctrine everything created was the work of the devil, a series of extremely severe obligations was imposed on the Perfect (i.e. on those fully initiated through *the consolamentum*). They were not allowed to eat meat or anything derived from animals—such as eggs, milk, cheese. This was immediately connected with their doctrine of metemphsychosis. The only exception was fish, in addition to which they allowed the use of wine, bread, oil, vegetables and fruit. Fasts were frequent and prolonged. Absolute chastity was, of course, rigorously imposed, since union with a woman could result in the procreation of a human being, a subject of Satan. Marriage was regarded as an abomination worse than concubinage, sodomy or even incest. Such aberrations were simply the logical consequences of Catharist premises, and the social danger of such a religion is self-evident. Apart from any considerations of a metaphysical or even moral kind, the increase in this sect constituted a danger to society.

The Catharists advocated anarchism, anti-militarism and communism. They also considered voluntary suicide as the ideal of perfection. The Believers received *the consolamentum* on their deathbeds, when there would be no further chance of recovery. However, if they happened to recover, they were encouraged to commit suicide, by taking poison, by opening their veins and bleeding to death in a bath, or, more frequently, by undergoing the *endura,* a hunger strike. The obvious purpose of this practice was to prevent the regenerated "believers" from defiling the ranks of the "perfect" in the event that they regained their health.

The Perfect were, of course, much less numerous than the Believers, but the doctrine, in spite of certain variations which divided the Cathari into, for example, Monarchians and Dualists, was the same for all. The simple believers were not bound by a morality as stringent as that imposed on the Perfect, but, since they equally despised marriage, it is clear into what excesses they were drawn. "The Believer," says Pierre Belperron, "was regarded as one who, having no hope of salvation in this life unless *the consolamentum* was eventually administered to him on his deathbed, could give himself full scope without any of his actions entailing any real consequence for him." Need we add that the knowledge of their own immeasurable superiority over the simple Believers and, *a fortiori,* over the rest of mankind, begot in the Perfect a monstrous pride born of their conviction that to them alone salvation was reserved. Since the sole condition for salvation was the reception of *the consolamentum,* the latter ultimately became the only religion of the Believer, who aspired to its reception either during his life or at the moment of death.

The Perfect devoted themselves to a sustained and intense apostolate, not only with a view to creating other Perfect through administering *the consolamentum* during life or at the hour of death to Believers, but also with the aim of winning over as many as possible of the faithful of the Catholic Church, which they re-

garded as the Scarlet Woman of the Apocalypse and
as the Synagogue of Satan.

Unhappily, this propaganda was listened to by the
masses. Some, desiring to reach the ranks of the Perfect, aspired to a life purified and in some sort wholly
spiritualized; others, while remaining attached to earth-
ly things, could not but make comparisons between
these same Perfect, commonly called "good men," and
the members of the Catholic clergy who were frequently very ignorant men leading a more or less
disedifying or scandalous life. In his fine works on
Albigensianism and the Inquisition in Languedoc, Jean
Guiraud, a conscientious historian, unhesitatingly de-
nounces the sad condition of Catholicism in southern
France when Saint Bernard's apostolic zeal brought
him there, and later when Saint Dominic founded there
his Order of Preachers. At that period, the Cistercian
Monks themselves, and especially the Abbots, traveled
about on richly caparisoned mules, making a display
of luxury which contrasted badly with the poverty
and lack of display characteristic of "the good men."
The lower clergy, often molested at the instigation of
the Cathari, were not only discouraged by a knowledge
of their own powerlessness, but even inclined to make
the best of their poor lot by establishing good relations
with the heretics themselves, thereby making it extremely difficult for them to convince these heretics
of the error of their ways.

The heresy infiltrated to such an extent that there
were adherents of the sect even in certain religious
houses. Jean Guiraud cites the almost incredible example of a Dominican of the Priory of Prouille who,
in the time of Saint Dominic himself, became a mem-

ber; and there is every evidence to show that the evil
was great among the secular clergy. The heresy had
won over the upper classes, so that this or that great
lord—for example the Count of Toulouse—while making
a show of submission to the Church, would more or less
openly favor it. Furthermore, since the Perfect exercised a real social action helping the poor to learn
a trade and showing themselves both charitable and
generous, their success with the people grew more and
more.

In southern France there were three Catharist
churches, in Albi, Toulouse and Carcassonne, besides
less important centers such as Agen and Le Razes. At
the head of these churches was a Bishop with two
assistants, one of whom automatically succeeded on
the death of the Bishop. To prevent any dispute about
succession, it was customary for the Bishop to consecrate in advance the one chosen ultimately to succeed
him. The Bishop was assisted by Deacons, itinerants
who administered the possessions which their Church
had need of, even though the Perfect themselves prac-
tised an absolutely rigorous poverty.

Though they had not priories nor convents properly
so called, the Perfect often lived a community life in
houses belonging to the sect. There they would receive
those who aspired to receive *the consolamentum*, and
the daughters of noble families affiliated to Catharism.

We must not be blinded to the lethal danger of the
Albigensian heresy by admiration for the moral strictness of the Perfect, or by sympathy at reading the
brutal manner of repression during the Simon de
Montfort crusade. Had the heresy succeeded, it is not
the Church alone that would have been persecuted

and rendered unable to fulfill its mission; according to C. H. Lea, a writer who is scarcely suspect of any tender feelings towards Catholicism, the triumph of this heresy would have reduced Europe to the savage conditions of a primitive age. For this heresy, says Lea, was more than a revolt against the Church: it was man's abdication of his own nature.

In twelfth and thirteenth century Languedoc, besides the Cathari, we find another heresy which, though with fewer members, has unlike Albigensianism subsisted into our own age, having fused, however, with the Reformed religion in the sixteenth century. This is the sect of the Waldenses. The founder of the sect was Peter Waldes of Lyons, a rich banker. He was a pious man, devoted to the reading of the Scriptures which had been translated into the vernacular by two priests. With the assistance of a Canon of Lyons, he devoted himself to spreading among the people copies of the vernacular Gospels and of certain books of the Old Testament. The premature death of this Canon affected him so deeply that he sold all he possessed, gave the proceeds to the poor, and devoted himself to preaching. He gathered a body of disciples and sent them out to spread the Good Tidings. This group came to be known as the Humiliati or "Poor Men of Lyons." All this occurred in 1160, and it was only twenty years later that the ecclesiastical authorities became suspicious about them. Then the Archbishop of Lyons, Jean de Belles-Mains, forbade them to continue their activities. It seems clear that Peter Waldes regarded himself as still in union with the Church of Rome, since he appealed from the archiepiscopal sentence to Pope Lucius III, an appeal which the Pope nonsuited. As a result of this papal decision, Waldes, the precursor of Wycliff, Huss and Luther, summarily rejected the authority of the Church, and in consequence the exclusive right of the clergy to preach publicly the word of God.

Very soon, the "Poor Men of Lyons" became a sect whose French branch was restricted to the valleys of the Alps and Piedmont, with headquarters at Torre Pellice. (The Italian branch—the *Poor Lombards*—had spread extensively in Germany, Bohemia and Poland.) According to prevailing circumstances or the whim of the Prince, the rulers of Savoy treated them tolerantly or harshly. In southern France, where this heresy showed a tendency to propagate itself jointly with that of the Cathari, it seems that there were certain correspondences between the two sects, though the Waldenses were fundamentally the less dangerous. Like the orthodox Protestants of our day, they seem to have been Christians solely preoccupied with a return to the religion of the first disciples of Christ. They had no liturgical worship. In the form of an imposition of hands, they too received a *consolamentum*, designed to secure for them the effusion of the Holy Spirit, a ceremony in the course of which they undertook their obligations for the future. On Holy Thursday, one of their elders celebrated a rite very similar in type to the Calvinist 'Lord's supper;' he consecrated bread and wine—without, however, believing in the Real Presence—and distributed them to the faithful.

When the followers of Peter Waldes began to spread into Languedoc, the Catholic people, far from suspecting them of heresy, admired and welcomed them as authentic Christians. In its early period in southern France, the Inquisition paid little heed to the Waldenses. Later however, at the end of the thirteenth century, when Albigensianism had been successfully dealt with, greater attention was given to the "Poor Men of Lyons," a number being arrested, questioned and condemned.

All historians are unanimous that the essential reason for the amazing proliferation of heresy in southern France was the lax condition of the clergy. The bishops belonged to noble families, and were very much more concerned about the collection of revenue than about the salvation of souls. Berenger, Archbishop of Narbonne, is a case in point. Thirteen years after his election, he had not yet visited his diocese, and he had demanded the payment of a very large sum as his price for consecrating the Bishop of Maguelonne, his suffragan. If it chanced that a bishop more energetic than his fellows attempted to preach publicly against the Albigenses, the people rose against him. For instance, Berenger, Bishop of Carcassonne—not to be confused with Berenger of Narbonne—was molested by the Catholics themselves and forced to leave the town.

Besides, many of those bishops who owed their election to the patronage of the Counts of Toulouse, had family connections, often very close, with the Albigenses. This was equally true of the monastic abbots—men who very often devoted themselves to hunting parties and to other pastimes incompatible with their dignity and their calling. There were also certain parish priests who attended the sermons of these heretics and even brought their parishioners to hear them. In such conditions, there is no longer any mystery about the case with which the Albigenses got a hearing from the people when they thundered against the bad behavior of the clergy and against the ecclesiastical abuses of the times.

CHAPTER THREE

Intervention by the Church Establishment of the Inquisition

Despite the extreme slowness of communications in the age with which we are dealing, the Popes did not neglect to keep in touch with conditions in the various regions of the Church. As early as the sixth century, we find Saint Gregory the Great vehemently reproaching the Archbishop of Cagliari who, among others, was guilty of neglecting the evangelization of a still pagan population in central Sardinia; and how much easier is it for us, therefore, to accept the fact that, in the latter part of the twelfth century, the Popes were alarmed by the lamentable conditions of the Church in southern France, the corruption of the clergy there, and the progress made by the most dangerous of heresies.

In 1145, a Pisan, Cardinal Bernard Paganelli, former Cistercian and Abbot of Saints Vincent and Anastasius in Rome, became Pope Eugene III. The successor of Lucius II was a beloved disciple of Saint Bernard, who now became his most valued adviser. A few months after the accession of Eugene III, Saint Bernard made his journey into Languedoc, where he found matters in a very serious condition, for the reasons we have already outlined. The two most active propagandists of the heresy had been a certain Pierre de Bruys, a kind of precursor of the Waldenses, and a wandering monk about whom little is known beyond the fact that he was called Henri of Lausanne. Having wandered from town to town and been obliged to flee from Mans where the Bishop had put him to silence, he had reached Toulouse where he was leading many Catholics astray. He was still there in 1145 when Saint Bernard arrived, called to Languedoc by the Papal Legate, Alberic, Cardinal Archbishop of Ostia, monk of Cluny. A twofold task awaited the saint: to work for the reform of the clergy and for the conversion of the heretics.

Saint Bernard preached successively at Toulouse and Albi, but he was prevented from doing so at Verfeil. He placed the Abbey of Grandselve under the Citeaux obedience, in order that, by their example and their activity, the monks of his Order might be a leaven to reform and to transform the clergy. Though he accomplished outstanding miracles, especially in Toulouse, and his eloquence proved effective in galvanizing the multitude, it cannot be said that his mission fully accomplished its purpose. The evil was too deep. Nevertheless, the Church's zeal for its extirpation did not diminish. The Council of Tours, at which Pope Alexander III presided in person, solemnly condemned the "damnable heresy" with which Toulouse and Gascogne were deeply infected. The Hierarchy of southern France, in general assembly at Lombez, probably in 1178, uttered a new condemnation, which had no effect on the situation.

At that time—that is, in the Pontificate of Alexander III (1159-1181) and the reign of Louis VII—a crusade was envisaged and this a long time before it was actually to be carried out. In spite of the meager results obtained by Saint Bernard more than thirty years earlier, the Pope, reluctant to use force, preferred to send a new mission into Languedoc. We have, therefore, many years before its official institution, an adumbration of the Inquisition. The mission was headed by a Papal Legate, Peter, Cardinal of Saint Chrysogonus. He was assisted by a certain number of Prelates— the Archbishop of Bourges, the Bishop of Poitiers, the Abbot of Citeaux, and the Bishop of Bath (England).

The representatives of the Holy See installed themselves at Toulouse under the protection of Count Raymond V and under the more powerful protection of the King of France. The results obtained by this mission seem to have been rather slight, and the sanctions were limited to a certain number of sentences of excommunication. There was no question of appeal to the secular arm. The determination to make this appeal was to come the following year at the ecumenical Lateran Council (1179), at which the Cathari or "Patarins" of Gascogne and the Albigensians were specifically named and where it was decided that, to render these heresies powerless to spread evil, recourse could be had to the support of the secular powers.

The mission to Languedoc was strengthened and Henri, Abbot of Clairvaux, was put in charge. During the Pontificate of Lucius III, successor of Alexander III, the Legate was created Cardinal Bishop of Albano. He had both energy and zeal, but the exterior circumstances were far from favorable. Trouble in Italy diverted the attention of Celestine III—Lucius III had died in 1185—from southern France, where the Catharist heresy was now spreading with renewed vigor.

The year 1198 saw the election of a young Pope, a man with a deep sense of the supereminent grandeur of the Roman Pontificate, whose accession was to mark the beginning of a new era in many domains, among them that of the repression of heresy. Cardinal Lothario of Segni, as Pope Innocent III (1198-1216), was to prove himself one of the greatest Popes in history, and if he was not the one who explicitly instituted the Inquisition, he certainly prepared the way for his successor, Gregory IX, who created and codified it. On the other hand, the name of Innocent III is inseparable from that of the Crusade against the Albigenses.

In the first place, it must be remembered that Innocent III originated the preaching of Saint Dominic in the Narbonnaise, this preaching being closely connected in its turn with the foundation of the Order of Friars Preachers. In 1203, the Pope had conferred very extensive powers on his two Legates in Languedoc, Peter of Castelnau and Raoul, both Cistercians of the Abbey of Fontfroide. In January 1204, Innocent III issued a Bull, in which he detailed the different kinds of activity demanded of the official representatives of the Holy See for the extirpation of heresy in Gaul

Narbonnaise. One of the most urgent concerns of the
Pope was to multiply preachers who, in the manner
of missionaries in pagan lands, would travel about
the country for the conversion of those led astray by
heresy.

These steps taken by Innocent III coincided with
the return to Rome of the Bishop of Osma, Diego de
Acebes. He had been sent to Denmark by Alphonsus
IX, King of Castille, to arrange a royal marriage with a
young princess there. The Bishop returned with the
news that the girl had died. The effect of this sad
incident on Diego was that he wanted to resign his
See and to devote himself to the evangelization of
the Kumans of southern Russia. During his *ad limina*
visit to Rome, he was accompanied by a small group
of collaborators, most prominent among them being
Dominic de Guzman, sub-prior of his Cathedral chapter. Innocent III immediately realized the value of
the help which Providence was offering him. He refused the resignation of Diego de Acebes, and directed
him to consecrate himself, not to the conversion of
the Kumans, but to that of the heretics who were
multiplying in southern France. The affair was particularly opportune, as the Pope had just then received
bad news from Languedoc. His Legate, Peter of Castelnau, had confided his utter discouragement to the
Pope. The Cistercians were monks more suited to con-
templation than to the active ministry then and there
urgently required. The Pope turned especially to Dominic, a man younger than Bishop Diego who praised
him highly to Innocent. This young man, who on his
journey had converted his Catharist host at Toulouse,

had all the requisite qualities for the mission whose success was the Pope's ardent wish.

The Spanish Pilgrims left Rome, therefore, late in 1204, and began their task by visiting Citeaux in order to make sure that missionaries would be sent to them after they themselves, that is, Diego and Dominic, had prepared the way.

The Bishop of Osma and Dominic met the Papal Legates at Montpellier and arranged with them the forms the mission was to take. The Spaniards began by suggesting to the Cistercians that they should lay aside all their extravagant trappings and set about the evangelization of the country by giving an example of truly apostolic poverty. Shortly afterwards, Diego died in his Castille diocese of Osma, to which he had returned in quest of support for the mission. Dominic established himself at Fanjeaux, and the Bishop of Toulouse conceded to him the Church of Notre-Dame of Prouille, close to which he instituted a religious house for the purpose of receiving women and girls, mostly of noble families, won over from heresy. In a sense that religious house can be regarded as the cradle of the Order of Friars Preachers. In the official documents of the time, it was even called "La Sainte Predication."

We have reached 1207. Henceforth, Dominic de Guzman had a general headquarters whence his influence spread through the country in the eight following years which coincided with the Albigensian crusade. Foulque, Bishop of Toulouse, whose apostolic zeal contrasted with the scandalous weakness of a great number of his fellow bishops, was the first to institute in his diocese missionaries bound by a rule of life, who were soon highly successful. They were Dominic's collaborators. Their renown spread abroad, and, in the course of the Fourth Ecumenical Lateran Council (The Twelfth Ecumenical Council, 1215), Pope Innocent III approved their rule of life.

Thus, this new Religious Order, which was to become so closely associated with the later function of the Inquisition, was connected in its origins with the repression of the Albigensian heresy. While the barons of the north were combating that heresy by force, Dominic, with a wholly evangelical approach was converting a very great number of heretics by his prayer and preaching.

This apostolic activity of Saint Dominic and his companions in the Toulouse region slightly preceded the Crusade. It continued in the fringe of these hostilities which lasted from 1209 until 1226, and with sporadic outbreaks until 1271.

From all that we have outlined here, we can appreciate the set of circumstances through which such a court as the Inquisition could come into existence, and why it was that it should function in southern France before being extended to other countries. Certain writers have regarded Dominic as the first Grand Inquisitor. This is entirely false. Whatever the zeal of the founder of the Friars Preachers in detecting, fighting and extirpating the Albigensian heresy in southern France, at no time did he discharge functions similar to those of the later Thomas de Torquemada in Spain.

The source of this error concerning Dominic is as follows. While the Inquisition properly so called was organized and codified by Gregory IX in 1231—that is, ten years after the death of Saint Dominic—this Pope was simply giving an official and *de jure* existence to an institution which already existed *de facto*. Gregory IX was none other than the celebrated Cardinal Ugolino, nephew of Innocent III and friend and protector of Saint Francis and Saint Dominic. He had known and esteemed the companionship of the Bishop of Osma during their visit to Rome, and indeed it was at his house that the two founders were able to meet for long discussions.

However novel the form of religious life adopted by Francis and Dominic and founded on the principle of absolute poverty, Cardinal Ugolino had understood better than anyone else the full import and value of this kind of social and ecclesiastical revolution. Freed from all the restrictions of a monastic life, the religious mendicants, by reason of their itinerant way of life, were able to mix more intimately with the people and to exercize a deep and salutary influence, especially over the lower ranks of society.

It is not surprising, therefore, that Dominicans and Franciscans were used very soon to fight against heresy and to stem its diffusion through all classes of society.

The abuses committed by the Crusaders under Simon de Montfort, who had come from the north after the murder of Papal Legate Peter de Castelnau by an equerry of Count Raymond VI of Toulouse, created the danger that the innocent would suffer as well as the guilty. Consequently, in the Pontificate of Innocent III, it became necessary to legislate about the punishments to be imposed on heretics.

The Fourth Lateran Council (1215) saw to this. Formal heretics were to be handed over to the civil power; ecclesiastics were to be deposed and their possessions given to the churches to which they had been attached; the goods of the laity were to be confiscated. A person merely suspected of heresy who could not justify himself was to be excommunicated for a year, after which he would be regarded as a formal heretic if he continued unrepentant. An obligation was placed on rulers to eliminate heretics from their territories: if they neglected this obligation, they could be excommunicated and, after a lapse of one year, removed from their office.

The death penalty did not figure, however, in this legislation of Innocent III. Nevertheless, in certain circumstances and on several occasions, especially in western Germany, the people had passed summary sentence on the guilty and had condemned them to the stake. In Spain, King Pedro II of Aragon had declared heretics to be public enemies and had ordered *autos da fe*. Frederick II, whose own orthodoxy was highly suspect, had ordered sever punishments because of the spread of the heresy in northern Italy. The guilty person was to be made an example of, by having his tongue cut out or by being burnt alive. These corporal punishments—laid down, be it remembered, by the civil authority—found their justification in Roman law.

Up to that time, bishops had been free to act as they saw fit within their own dioceses. However, in 1231, Gregory IX, a man of great energy and decision despite his very advanced age, set about standardizing the regulations in force in different countries for the suppression of heretics. Having been first published by the Senator, the supreme magistrate of the Holy City, these new statutes came into force in Rome, after which immediate steps were taken to establish them everywhere else.

Here a question arises with an essential bearing on the later development of the Inquisition. While the Church has a horror of blood, she has also a lively concern for justice. She must, of course, guard the purity of the Faith and see that the faithful are not contaminated by error, but she is also concerned to make necessary discriminations so that the innocent are not punished with the guilty. Up to this time, this had been a matter confided to the bishops, but Gregory IX now sought to prevent any arbitrary behavior in this domain. He commenced his new policy in Germany by appointing to the task of detecting heretics the highly worthy but extremely severe priest, Conrad of Marburg, confessor to Saint Elizabeth of Hungary, assisted by educated and competent ecclesiastics.

In Sicily, where Frederick II prosecuted heresy as a crime of treason, it was to civil officers of state that the Emperor issued the order and the necessary instructions for dealing with the guilty. His aims were much more political than religious. Opposition to the Empire was strong in the Lombard towns and there were also numerous heretics in those towns. Hence the severity of the corrupt Frederick towards the heterodox: his instructions were that they should be burnt alive in the public squares in the presence of the people.

Gregory IX could certainly not disapprove the war against heresy, but, on the other hand, he equally could not admit the principle by which the task of seeking out heresy would be confided to lay and incompetent functionaries. That was why he appointed inquisitors directly dependent on and holding their mandates from the Holy See. Conrad of Marburg proved to be the exceptional case, for no other secular priest was chosen; it became the accepted practice to appoint Franciscans and Dominicans, especially Dominicans, to the office of Inquisitor.

The Inquisitor had now an official existence, and it was only a question of providing it with solid juridical foundations. Hence the concern of Gregory IX to regulate inquisitorial procedure. An order was given that all those who considered themselves guilty of heresy were to present themselves before the court of the Inquisition, which, in its turn, was to persuade them of their error and lead them to repentance. A period of delay, known as "the time of grace," was allowed in the case of those presumed guilty. This period was generally one month, during which sermons would be preached to enable each person to make a severe examination of conscience. After that, the Inquisitor heard evidence and denunciations which he would register, whatever their source, even if they came from heretics. Two denouncers were required for the accused to be presumed guilty, provided he did not successfully refute the accusations.

If the accused admitted his guilt and showed repentance a penance was imposed on him of a gravity proportionate to the fault; for example, the recitation of certain prayers, the undertaking of a fast or a pilgrimage, the undergoing of a (generally purely symbolic) public flogging. If the crime was great, however, he could be condemned to wear a yellow cross on his clothes or to undergo a term of imprisonment. He would be handed over to "the secular arm" only if he persisted obstinately in his grave error. It should be noticed, moreover, that, according to the exact researches carried out by Msgr. Douai and Jean Guiraud, and even by a hostile writer like Lea, only exceptionally was a sentence passed handing the condemned to "the secular arm" with the consequent risk of execution.

A verdict of the Court of the Inquisition could not be pronounced without all necessary guarantees having been provided for the accused. In the early stages of its existence, the Inquisitor was assisted by a bishop or by a bishop's representative. Later, he was surrounded by experts, men of irreproachable life highly versed in the law—the *boni viri* who adumbrated the Jury instituted in medieval England and introduced into France by the Revolution.

The Inquisitor could not pronounce sentence without having consulted his assistants. The accused appeared before the Court as a completely free man. Preventive imprisonment was unknown. He had one or several defenders, that is to say, an attorney and a procurator who, like the assessors or *boni viri*, had to be persons of known and sufficient integrity. When sentence was pronounced, the condemned had the right to appeal to Rome, a right he would certainly use, since he could thus prolong his case, apart altogether from the fact that the Courts of the Holy See were known to be more indulgent than local ones.

There remains the question of torture, the question par excellence concerning the Inquisition. We have seen that the Court had been officially instituted in 1231 by Gregory IX. Some twenty years later, Innocent

IV promulgated the constitution *Ad extirpanda* (May 15, 1252) creating a number of regulations relative to the functioning of the Inquisition. One of the articles of this document authorized the inquisitorial Court to hand over for torture by a representative of the civil power, any person presumed guilty. It was specified that there should be no mutilation of the accused as a result, and that his life should not be endangered.

It was not permitted, says the text, "to cut off a member or to torture the accused to the point of death." We must remember that such measures were current practice at that time; they had their origin in Roman Law and in certain of the Germanic legal systems. In a reply to a request, in the ninth century, by the converted Boris, ruler of Bulgaria, for priests, Pope Nicholas I (858-867) protested vigorously against the use of torture which, he said, ran counter to both divine and human law. These noble sentiments had not prevailed. It was only in modern times, towards the end of the eighteenth century, that the Milan lawyer, Cesare Beccaria, destroyed this legacy of barbarism by creating a current of opinion by which it was ultimately swept away.

In the early stages of the Inquisition, the Inquisitors could not assist at the torture, but later, about 1260, this prohibition was rescinded on the grounds that a heretic might recant when given "the question." He was then condemned to perpetual imprisonment. Only the recidivist and the obstinate were condemned to the flames. If a person was posthumously convicted of heresy, his body was disinterred and burned, and his goods were confiscated.

Although the Popes made laws about the functioning of the Inquisition, which were to be added to the codes of different countries, the application of those laws nevertheless varied from region to region. In northern Italy, despite the severe prescriptions of Frederick II, it was considered sufficient to banish heretics. On the other hand, an extreme severity was the rule in Germany: Conrad de Marburg had a great number   condemned to the flames. He ended by being himself a victim to the fury of the people.

The example of Conrad de Marburg was one of the factors which led to the appointment of the Franciscans and Dominicans to implement the Court of the Inquisition. Without a fixed residence, constantly on the move, immune from those local influences which could be brought to bear on permanently located judges, the Franciscans and Dominicans formed, so to speak, an ubiquitous militia in constant and direct contact with the Holy See, and able to discover the most concealed heresy, thanks to the immediate contact which these men had with all classes of society. Furthermore, this heresy, then so widespread, was an insidious evil.

In our time, Catholics and Protestants can live side by side anywhere in Christendom without a thought of dissimulating the religion to which they belong. In medieval times, when the very idea of tolerance was unknown, it was often a difficult matter to recognize heretics, however numerous they might be in a particular region. Jean de Meung, in the *Roman de la Rose,* chose to portray the mendicant Friars as dissimulators; but in reality the name could have been more aptly applied to those heretics—Catharists, Patarins, Lollards, Waldenses—who exteriorly professed Catholicism while being secretly its worst enemies. They were victims, it is said, of an odious persecution on the part of priests and monks. But how would they themselves have behaved had they gained complete control! In opposing the contamination of the faithful by the most pernicious of errors, the Church was defending society itself and the whole of Christian civilization.

In southern France, the Crusade against the Albigenses had had the effect of making the heretics more subtle in their behavior rather than of ending the heresy itself. In a later chapter, we shall meet a phenomenon of a similar kind in connection with the Spanish Inquisition and the marranos.

The first problem, therefore, was to find the heretics, and oath-taking was one means of doing so. According to the Cathari, it was a grave sin to take an oath. If therefore someone came before the Court, even as a witness, and refused to take the oath, this fact alone would give a strong presumption that he was affiliated with the sect.

Anyone suspected of heresy was obliged to justify and to purge himself, on pain of losing his civil rights and of incurring excommunication. Gradually the power and prerogatives of the Inquisition increased considerably. Apart from heresy, the Inquisitors prosecuted certain crimes—for example, usury, a practice condemned by the Bible. Since it was forbidden to act as witness in favor of the heretic, a testament, to be valid, had to be drawn up before someone affiliated with the Inquisition.

Unlike the practice among nobles and high ecclesiastical dignitaries, the Inquisitors did not put on a show of pomp when they appeared in public. They preferred to work in shadow and silence, behind the walls of the Holy Office. They could operate only with the help of many secret agents appointed to discover and to denounce those presumed to be guilty. The Inquisitor whose seat was in the chief town of the region where he exercised his functions, would go from place to place at certain times, assemble the faithful, preach in praise of the true faith, denounce heresy, and enjoin the faithful to report within twelve days whatever they knew, on pain of excommunication for failing in this duty.

During a period not exceeding one month, the heretic could come forward of his own accord and confess and renounce his error, with full assurance that he would be treated with leniency. The quality of the leniency was at the discretion of the Inquisitor. The repentant person might get a free pardon, or be condemned to exile, to loss of goods, to a public penance, or to a pilgrimage. A pilgrimage at that time was often a dangerous undertaking and always a very exhausting one. When the period of penance had elapsed, the known heretic could no longer count on the leniency of the Inquisitorial Court.

Here the imperial historian meets with one stumbling block which he cannot ignore. We have already pointed out that the spread of dangerous heretical doctrines, especially of those derived from the Manicheans, constituted an extreme danger for the temporal and social stability of the state as well as for the Church and for the salvation of souls. In the Middle

Ages, we have said, heresy of any kind was regarded as treason against the Divine Majesty. The civil power, closely linked with the religious authority (despite clashes between them from time to time), equally denied to its subjects any right to hold heterodox doctrines. To the extent to which heresy was regarded as a social danger—and Albigensianism was, in fact, a great one—the Church was bound to intervene. This important point must be kept in mind if an objective idea is to be formed of the nature of the medieval Inquisition. This being understood, however, the method of repression cannot fail to be a thorny problem.

In our time, we see and have seen even worse, but we are not to justify past abuses which the Church more or less sanctioned, by appealing to the example given today by her embittered enemies. Now, what shocks us in the procedure of the Inquisitors, even if they could have acted otherwise, is that the service of informers (delation) was the foundation of their system. This would not have been so bad if zeal for the purity of the faith had always been the motive for denouncing a relative, a friend, an acquaintance, even an enemy. But what a temptation this offered to the ignorant and the spiteful to denounce simply through vindictiveness or for revenge!

Obliged as he was to judge in accordance with denunciations often difficult to assess, the Inquisitor needed to be a man of uncommon intelligence and strength of character. Before the man who could pardon them or have them burned at the stake, the accused had to undergo an interrogation, where the intellectual odds were very much against them, by an educated man and a theologian versed in all the subtleties of dialectics.

All this constitutes a very real dilemma. On the one hand, the Church had to take every means to extirpate heresy; on the other hand, in order to uncover heresy, she had to use methods which tended too easily to throw suspicion on those who might very well have been innocent. However exaggerated the number of victims attributed to the Inquistion, one cannot applaud the system of information-gathering on which it based its activity.

CHAPTER FOUR

Development of the Inquisition

We have seen that the episcopal Inquisition preceded the one instituted by Pope Gregory IX and
confided, with direct mandate from the Holy See, to
the Dominicans and Franciscans. This does not mean
that the Popes sought to abolish the episcopal Inquisition and to deprive the bishops of a right which, in a
sense, was inherent in their mission. Nevertheless, although in principle no inquisitorial court could sit without authorization from the Ordinary of the diocese,
it was inevitable that a certain rivalry should develop
between the two jurisdictions, and that the Papal
Inquisitors should tend to behave as though they
were in fact fully independent.

When this happened, it was the Popes themselves
who drew up regulations to safeguard the episcopal
authority. In 1254, Innocent IV directed that the Bishop
must be consulted before sentences of death or of

perpetual imprisonment were pronounced. He also laid down that doubtful points should be interpreted by the Bishop and the Papal Inquisitor, acting together. A retrograde step was taken, however, in the Pontificate of Alexander IV, successor to Innocent IV, when the new Pope sought to give complete independence to the Inquisition by dispensing the Inquisitors from the duty of consulting the Ordinary, even in the case of fully convicted heretics.

This ignoring of episcopal authority could not last. In 1262, Urban IV drew up new instructions imposing the obligation to consult the bishop before pronouncing a sentence that could involve the death penalty or even life imprisonment. Shortly afterwards, in 1273, Gregory X again confirmed the necessity for consultation between the episcopal authority and the Papal Inquisitor.

This reminder, frequently renewed by the Popes, about the respect due to the spiritual head of a region in which a direct representative of the Holy See was operating, shows their constant concern to surround with all desirable guarantees the administration of justice in regard to the repression of heresy.

A similar concern lay behind the institution of the experts or *boni viri*, of whom we have already spoken. These experts were many, and they included a large percentage of lawyers. When a fixed number of cases had been examined, the accused duly questioned, the evidence heard and collated, the sentence had to be pronounced publicly in the course of a *sermo* or *auto da fe* (literally: act of faith, a public profession of faith), which took place always on a Sunday. There was a preliminary convocation of experts on the previous Friday. Each case was read out to them, but without the name of the accused being announced. The *boni viri*, who had sworn on the Bible to preserve secrecy and to judge in accordance with conscience and the guidance God would give them, then decided on the sentence for that case. The sentence would vary according to the gravity of the crime. It could be a penance to be decided by the Inquisitor, or life imprisonment, or abandonment to the secular arm— which usually meant the death sentence.

If the conclusions of the experts were modified by the Inquisitors, as frequently happened, the modification was towards greater leniency. Clearly, the whole pattern of procedure was dictated by a great concern to avoid injustice; and yet, there were inherent disadvantages. The care to preserve the utmost secrecy about the identity of the accused people meant that the assessors, the *boni viri*, faced with abstract cases, were led to give judgment and to pronounce sentence equally *in abstracto*. The aim of this anonymity was to prevent the experts from being influenced by personal or sentimental considerations concerning a particular accused person; but, on the other hand, their ignorance of the behavior of the accused, of his reactions, of the motives which actuated him, could lead them astray or incline them towards excessive severity. In this connection, the Abbe Vacandard rightly observes: "The Courts are to judge criminals, not crimes, just as doctors treat patients and not diseases. If the treatment for the same disease must vary from patient to patient according to the condition of each, a crime may be equally regarded in different ways according to the mentality of those who have committed it. The Inquisition did not base itself on these principles."

Apart from those cases, happily rare, in which the accused was handed over to the secular arm and therefore condemned to death, the concern of the Popes was always to secure a mitigation of the sentences pronounced. One sentence was that of perpetual imprisonment, which meant, in the expression of the time, that the condemned was "to be immured for the rest of his days." Although this epoch was characterized by widespread crudity of manners, it does not necessarily follow that the prisoners were invariably subjected to the regime of "the bread of sorrow and the water of anguish." Since the goods of the condemned had been confiscated, it was the bishop's duty to draw upon those goods for whatever was necessary to secure suitable treatment for the condemned person. The heretic being regarded as a danger to his fellow citizens, prison was the surest means of isolating him and of preventing the contagion of error.

Impartial historians are agreed that, on the whole, the conditions in which these prisoners lived were pretty liberal. We must not be misled by the word "immured," meaning "surrounded by walls." In the course of their captivity, many of the condemned enjoyed a relative freedom which would have been appreciated by Silvio Pellico and his companions of the Spielberg, or by the victims of this century's concentration camps. However, it was always a question of the individual case. This or that prisoner was given permission to return home to nurse his sick father, or simply because he had asked. On the other hand, the prison cells, which were theoretically supposed not to be such as to injure the prisoner's health, were in reality dark and airless holes, in which the unfortunates, more than half starved, crouched in their own ordure and were unable to move about.

Against such abuses, the Popes had again to take steps. Clement V, the first Avignon Pope, gave instructions that the prisons were to be kept in good order, under the direct surveillance of the bishop and of the Inquisitor, that the prisoners were to be decently fed, and that provisions intended for a particular prisoner were to reach him intact. Not content with just ordering these measures, Clement V insisted that they were carried out. He sent Legates who visited the prisons of Albi and Carcassonne and saw to it that the fetters were removed and that prisoners were taken out of their underground holes.

We must now deal with an even more delicate point: the general behavior of the Popes and the Papal Inquisitors in the cases where the condemned was delivered to the secular arm and had to die at the stake. While it is a fact that, in certain places, the attitude of the people themselves was one of violence towards the heretics, it was perhaps more often the case that the townspeople in places where the Inquisitors exercised their functions showed no inclination to second their efforts. We have already noted the merciless cruelty with which the Emperor Frederick II had prescribed the hunting down and the extirpation of heresy in the Lombard cities where it was widespread. Faced with the evident reluctance of the civil authorities when asked to second the efforts of the Inquisition, the Popes were several times forced to resort to the menace of interdiction against disobedient

towns and of excommunication against deliberately
negligent magistrates.

Already, in 1184, at the Council of Verona, Pope
Lucius III had ordered rulers to take an oath to
carry out conscientiously the ecclesiastical and civil
laws binding them to the repression of heresy. This
oath was to be taken in the presence of the bishops.
Undoubtedly, these prescriptions were not observed
to the letter, and in 1252 we find Pope Innocent IV
issuing a new and still more severe decree: "When
any persons have been condemned for heresy, by the
Bishop, by his Vicar, or by the Inquisitors, and delivered to the secular arm, the *podesta* or governor of
the city must take them in charge immediately and,
within five days, apply the laws which have been in-
voked against them." This extract is taken from the
famous Bull *Ad Extirpanda*, which, with the edicts of
Frederick II, was to be inserted in the constitutions of
the cities. Now these imperial edicts, whose rigorous
application the Pope was demanding, contained the
death sentence for heretics, condemned to be burned
alive.

At the end of the thirteenth century, Popes Clement
IV and Nicholas IV were to renew the prescriptions of
Innocent IV. According to these Pontifical measures,
the magistrate, into whose power was committed a
heretic condemned as such by the ecclesiastical Court,
had to carry out his execution without delay under pain
of incurring an excommunication which would make
the magistrate himself a heretic if, after a lapse of
one year, it had not been lifted. In such a case, the
magistrate would himself be liable to the death sentence; whence for him the absolute and imperative

necessity of carrying out, in the name of the civil power, a verdict implied in that pronounced by the Church.

Although, in the preceding chapter, we have already dealt with the question of torture, we must return to the subject since it is complementary to what has just been said concerning the prescriptions of Innocent IV and their confirmation by two of his successors. In the Middle Ages, an accused could not be pronounced guilty until he had admitted his guilt. This was the origin of the constraint exercised on the accused in order that the judges might be able to say: *Habemus confitentem reum,* (We have a confessed criminal). Torture, we have said, has its roots in Roman Law and in Germanic law.

Long before the Inquisition, in order to establish the guilt or the innocence of the accused, or again, in cases of litigation, when one of the parties sought to prove his just claim, recourse was had to "the judgments of God." These were the famous ordeals—from the German *Urteil*—which were widely used in countries of Germanic origin. In an age when people lived in permanent contact, so to speak, with the supernatural, it is not surprising that, when faced with a doubt, they sought to get the truth through an appeal to the direct intervention of God.

There are precedents for this in the Old Testament, and, in the *Acts,* Saint Peter himself makes such an appeal, provoking the healing of a sick man or the death or Ananias and Saphira. Furthermore, many relics of pagan modes of thought still subsisted in the sixth and seventh centuries. Homer and Virgil constantly made the gods intervene in the lives of their heroes. Fully considered, while the ordeals were clearly the source of grave error and puerile illusions, they were nonetheless based on a laudable principle—the principle of a complete faith in Him Who said: "If you have faith as a grain of mustard seed, you shall say unto this mountain, remove hence to yonder place, and it shall remove."

The ordeals were of different kinds. There were the simple oath, the proof of the celebration of Mass by an accused priest or the reception of Holy Communion by a cleric in minor Orders or by a layman, the judiciary duel, the ordeal by fire, by the red hot iron, by boiling water, by cold water. The use made of these by the ecclesiastical, pontifical, episcopal and conciliar authorities varied considerably with time and place. It is not within our scope here to deal in detail with all the successive and often contradictory attitudes to the ordeals. It is sufficient for our purposes to recall that the ordeals were more readily admitted in the north than in the south—in other words, they flourished where the Germanic customs were still in force, whereas in Rome they were little used.

These strange practices became gradually more and more rare. The Fourth Lateran Council, under the Pontificate of Innocent III, forbade the representatives of the Church to have any part in them. It is nevertheless interesting to recall that in Florence, in 1498, Savonarola agreed to submit to the ordeal by fire in order to prove the justice of his cause against his Franciscan adversaries. A providential fall of rain prevented the strange ceremony from taking place, but we can see the whole matter as a survival of the ordeals such as they were practiced in bygone ages.

Appeals to the Judgments of God at least showed the desire to make truth prevail. They also pointed to the primitivity of the peoples of those ages. The use of torture was in certain respects connected with these ordeals, the distinction being, however, that here the accused himself freely agreed to undergo it. The Bull *Ad Extirpanda* of Innocent IV is the document authorizing the practice of subjecting to interrogation under torture an accused person who persistently refused to admit facts about which the Inquisition had strong presumptions amounting to quasi-certainty. Since preventive prison did not exist, the first constraint imposed on the alleged guilty person was precisely that of imprisonment. This was the *durus carcer* where the prisoner was put on a diet in order to break down his presumed obstinancy. His food was gradually diminished, for this, says Lea, "was regarded as one of the lawful and particularly effective means of bringing about a change of heart in the accused." According to the celebrated Inquisitor, Bernard Gui, this method was especially used in Languedoc.

If, however, it proved ineffectual, recourse would be had to the rack or to the strappado. The rack was a triangular trestle to which the accused's wrists and ankles were tied by cords which led to a jackscrew. When the screw was tightened, the limbs were excruciatingly stretched. The torture of the strappado consisted in hoisting him by a rope fastened to his wrists behind his back, and letting him fall to the length of the rope on to the ground. Less frequent was the torture of the accused by placing his feet, covered with grease, close to burning coals. This was resorted to, on certain occasions, for the interrogation of those presumed guilty of sorcery.

These are indeed odious practices. For a long time, the Inquisitor was forbidden to be present, but the prohibition was lifted because of complications ensuing from his absence. Torture was resorted to only as an ultimate measure when all other means of persuasion had failed, and only when there were very serious indications that the accused was guilty. When the Inquisitor accompanied the prisoner into the torture chamber, he continued to exhort him while he was being stripped for torture. The first session was confined to the milder types of torture, and care was taken to let the accused know about the gradations of severity in order to induce him to admit the charges made against him.

One's first valid reaction is that extorted confessions of this kind could have no legal value. There has been much debate, in our own times, about the validity of "spontaneous confessions" obtained by police methods. There can be no question, at all events, about confessions made under torture: they cannot, in conscience, be regarded as legitimate. The Inquisitors themselves realized this. It was laid down that a supplementary interrogation had to follow the interrogation under torture, the latter being confined strictly to half an hour. At any time, the accused could ask to make a confession, and if this occurred during torture, the torture ended at once. The accused was then taken to an adjoining room where his statement was written down and then read over to him in order that he might accept and sign it. Of course, this whole procedure was open to much abuse as is shown by the diligence with which Pope Clement V instituted enquiries into excesses committed by certain Inquisitorial Courts, notably that of Carcassonne. This concern of the Pope does him credit, and proves that if, after a long period of indulgence, the Church did resort to certain accepted practices derived from Roman Law, she nonetheless strove to mitigate the severity of judges whose own natural temperament inclined to excess.

Up to this point, we have dealt only with formal heretics as coming within the jurisdiction of the Inquisition. According to Saint Raymond of Penafort, "he who cut himself off from the faith of the Church" must be regarded as a heretic. According to Saint Thomas, who here echoes Saint Augustine, a heretic is one who obstinately cuts himself off, on a point of doctrine, from the faith of the Church—in other words, who continues to do so after the ecclesiastical authority had made him aware of his error. Gradually the idea of heresy took on a wider meaning. Schismatics could be regarded as heretics, because schism necessarily leads to heresy. Then came the case of the excommunicated who had not, within the space of a year, sought to have the sentence lifted. The purpose of this recrudescence of severity was to safeguard the authority of the Church, and especially that of the Pope. To disobey the Pope was to ignore his rights, and in consequence to fall into heresy.

The canonists of the period went on to regard the crime of superstition as akin to heresy. From this they passed on to usury. The Jews practiced usury, but as they were not baptized they could not be regarded as heretics. On the other hand, a Christian usurer could come into the hands of the Inquisition because he was transgressing a moral law which was part of ecclesiastical teaching. Finally, we come to those who indulged in magic and sorcery. At first, it was a matter of establishing some connection between heresy and the practices of the necromancers and sorcerers. Pope Alexander IV had even insisted on the necessity for establishing such a connection, in order that the Inquisition might be able to bring within its jurisdiction those who attended the witches' Sabbath. Subtle theologians eventually succeeded. There was a firm belief at that time that Satan or some other devil transported a person by night from one place to another, covering an enormous distance. Thomas de Cantimpre, biographer of Saint Albertus Magnus, reports a conversation between Albert and the Archbishop of Paris, in the course of which the famous Dominican related a similar case. The daughter of the Count of Schwalenberg, he said, had been carried away for several hours nightly by the devil.

In the attempts made to cure the intermittently mad Charles VI, in the fourteenth century, recourse was had to magical practices. Two Augustinians were authorized to use their incantations on the King, after they had alleged that they had the devils under their command. When they failed, they were publicly defrocked, and then handed over to the executioner to be decapitated and quartered. Three other magicians offered the same guarantees of success, and were burned alive for their failure. There was certainly no end to the popular belief in sorcery and in the direct intervention of demons in men's lives. Was not an old companion of Joan of Arc, Gilles de Rais, Marshal of France, condemned for sorcery in 1440? He was a man who led a double life and who in our times would be treated by psychiatry. His crimes, numerous and abominable it is true, were attributed to direct commerce with the devil. Since the crime of heresy could not be imputed to him, Gilles de Rais was not judged by the Inquisition, but by a secular court. He was condemned, and was hung before being given to the flames. Huysmans was fascinated by this strange figure of the criminal who died repentant: the hero, Durtal, of his novel, *La-Bas,* is presented as engaged in writing a life of Gilles de Rais.

The Inquisitors had definite theological guidance in dealing with cases of heresy, but their task was much less clearcut when they had to examine those accused of practicing sorcery. The Inquisition existed only to defend the purity of the faith against the contamination of heresy. In cases of magic and sorcery, the Inquisitors could intervene and judge only if the accused could be suspected of heresy. This provided a fine subject for dispute between the theologians, doctors of the Sorbonne, and high ecclesiastical dignitaries. The more enlightened among them regarded sorcerers and magicians simply as charlatans, no doubt capable of doing a lot of damage, but answerable to the civil courts and not to the Inquisition. Belief in the existence of magic was, in itself, they argued, a heresy of which the Inquisitors themselves would be guilty were they to credit such nonsense.

This opinion, undoubtedly an advance on the ideas of the time, did not prevail. The attitude adopted towards sorcery in the Middle Ages varied from country to country. In Spain, the religious authorities were extremely severe, perhaps because of Moorish influences to which Christians were constantly subject. In Germany, belief in spirits and the credence given to legends were so widespread that it would have been impossible to extirpate them without prosecuting half the population. In that case, the Inquisition showed greater prudence and indulgence than did the civil courts, and readily acquitted those accused of sorcery, merely ordering them to renounce the devil. There were even cases where a Bishop or an Inquisitor sought the help of a witch in his efforts to discover a heretic!

In England, and partially in Scotland, where belief in witches was very widespread, the clergy carried on an energetic campaign against superstition, with the result that there was little for the Inquisition to do in such matters. On the continent, however, inquisitorial activity in dealing with cases of magic, sorcery, bewitchment and other incantations, continued to increase. We shall return to this point when we are dealing with the case of the Templars.

It would take us too long to write in detail about sorcery and the Inquisition's part in dealing with it. One shudders at the thought of how many unfortunate men and women were tortured and burned alive for having "commerce with the devil." But these facts are inseparable from the harsh customs of the period.

CHAPTER FIVE

The Inquisition and the Templars

The affairs of the Knights Templars have been a subject of impassioned interest to many, and a rich source of ammunition against the Inquisition. We are concerned exclusively here with the role played by the ecclesiastical tribunal in this multi-ramified case. Thanks to a wealth of learned works, we have now a certain degree of knowledge about this obscure chapter of history, and we can better appreciate the Church's involvement in it.[1]

Let us say at the very outset that it is extremely difficult to reach an equitable and soundly based judgment about the affairs of the Templars. This monastic-military Order owed its origin to the Crusaders. In the period when Baldwin II was king of the short-lived Latin Kingdom of Jerusalem, Hugh of Payens and Godfrey of Saint-Omar, among other Knights, proposed that they should furnish the king with a kind of standing army in the form of an Order at once military and religious. The object was to secure the safety of the many pilgrims to the Holy Land. The Order derived its name (*Pauperes Commilitones Christi Templique Salomonici,* the Poor Militia of Christ and of Solomon's Temple) from the fact that Baldwin handed over to the Knights a part of his royal palace, the so-called "Temple of Solomon." Its first Grand Master, Hugh of Payens, obtained for it the approbation of the Council of Troyes in 1128. Clearly, there was nothing suspect about its origins. Saint Bernard of Clairvaux, who took such a lively interest in everything concerning the Crusade, a little later drew up a rule for this very original Order.

Its success was great. Vocations multiplied and the Knights covered themselves with glory in a great number of engagements. Nevertheless residence in a Muslim land necessarily entailed contacts which led to reciprocal understanding between the highly cultured people and the knights, with the latter developing ultimately an attitude of tolerance utterly foreign to France, to Germany, to Flanders, though something analogous to it existed in the court of Frederick II at Palermo and in the climate of the caliphats of Andalusia before the *Reconquista* liberation. Certain traces of this mentality can be found even in parts of *The Thousand and One Nights.* An Arab writer of the time, Oussma, cited by Rene Grousset in his monumental *Histoire des Croisades,* bears witness to this more civilized attitude: "There is not a single one of the newly arrived Franks who does not show himself more inhuman than his compatriots who are already established among us and on familiar terms with the

Moors." And later he adds: "Among the Franks, those
who have been long established among us and have
cultivated the society of the Moors, are far superior
to those who have recently come to join them."

These remarks apply especially to the Templars,
but also to the Knights Hospitallers founded about the
same time. And this is something that must be borne
in mind when one tries to fathom the extraordinary
fall of the Templars and the events which preceded
and determined their suppression.

During the terrible tragedy that led to the destruction of the Order, Nogaret brought a very serious
accusation against the Templars. According to him,
there was collusion between the Knights and the Moors.
However suspect the agent of the secret designs of
Philip the Fair, however odious the man who dared
to lay violent hands on the person of Pope Boniface
VIII, we must not consider as necessarily without
foundation the accusation he leveled against the Templars. Their long sojourn in Palestine, their constant
contact with the followers of Islam, the gradual refinement of their minds at a time when Western
Christians were still primitive and without nuance
or subtlety, had initiated them into a political science
and methods of government far in advance of the
West at that time.

Accordingly as the Templars grew in power and
in wealth, they assumed a position which we should
today call supra-national. Protectors of Christians in
the East, holders in time of enormous capitals,
bankers for many kings and princes or highly trust-
worthy administrators of their property, the Templars
dealt on a footing of equality with Emperors and kings.

They would even act as arbitrators in conflicts between the Holy See and the civil power. In the Near East, the Order had some fifteen fortified places with extensive land, each highly provisioned to support a siege and with a large staff, Moors to a great extent. They had Armenians and Turks in their service, and their hierarchy and interior organization were not without relationship with those of the Ismaelian sect whose all-powerful Master was the Old Man of the Mountain, Hassan, head of the Haschichins or *Assassins* whose exploits are at the root of the meaning of the latter word in several languages. Although a Moor, this Hassan, who posed as a kind of philosopher nourished on Greek thought, especially the ideas of the Sophists, was a perfect skeptic for whom God manifested Himself in the form of the universal Reason, generatrix of Knowledge. There was a certain connection between the theory of the Ismaelians and Gnosticism. We allude here to those more or less exotic beliefs because, as a result of the numerous contacts established between the Templars and the Eastern world, ideas held in milieux affiliated to Islam could not fail to influence these warrior monks gorged with riches and assimilated to a large extent with the East.

The Templars dreamed of a universal empire in which they would play a preponderant role; it would not be surprising, therefore, if they favored a certain syncretism derived from a fusion of Christian doctrine and the doctrine of Islam. We must remember that the Middle Ages were very given to universalist ideas. There was, for instance, Raymond Lull, raised to the Altar by the Church, who laid down the plan of the *Ars Generalis* aimed at converting the Muslims. Dante himself, in his *De Monarchia* and in many passages of *The Divine Comedy,* seems wholly impregnated with these universalist doctrines, which coalesce for him in the allegory of the Eagle and the Cross. As was certainly the case with Dante, the Templars had totally abandoned all national limitations. The Knight, whatever the degree of his initiation into the secret aims of the Temple, had to strive for the realization of this plan envisaging the supreme direction of human affairs and to do so under an obedience comparable only to that which was to exist later among the sons of Ignatius Loyola.

Philip the Fair at first cultivated the friendship of the Order, but only in order to use it for his own dynastic designs. He wanted his son to be appointed Grand Master, and when he failed to secure this, he dropped all pretense of friendship and became the implacable enemy of the Order. To achieve his new purpose of crushing the Templars and seizing their property, Philip found it necessary to secure the support of the Holy See, since he was dealing with an Order directly answerable to the Pope alone and with foundations in many countries where his Most Christian Majesty had no jurisdiction. Now, the imputation of heresy to the Templars was the one and only thing that would make the Church give satisfaction to Philip, and this was how the Inquisition came into the picture.

If Clement V had not been of a vacillating character and had not been suffering from what turned out to be a frightful cancer of the stomach, Philip the Fair would not have succeeded in his plan. The former Archbishop of Bordeaux, Bertrand de Got, who became Pope Clement V in 1305, was unable to take up residence

in Italy because disturbances were rife there, and had
to choose Avignon as his seat. This unfortunately put
him to a great extent in the power of the French
king, who constantly threatened to institute posthu-
mous proceedings against Boniface VIII whom Philip
accused of having been a heretic and a false Pope.
Without this oppressive concourse of circumstances,
the trial of the Templars would never have occurred;
never on his own initiative would Clement V have
taken action against the religious militia of which
Jacques de Molay was the Grand Master nor would
he ever have envisaged the suppression of the Order.

It still remained to collect evidence against the
Templars sufficient to give an apparent justification to
their arrest, torture and condemnation. Once again,
the principal agent was William of Nogaret. With
devilish cunning, he knew how to mix the false with the
true, seizing on matters that had a degree of probability
and even of truth, only to use them as a cover for the
most infamous calumnies, especially of a moral kind,
and for absurd fabrications, the most extravagant being that the Templars had not only renounced Christ
but were worshipping an idol which they called Baphomet.

The plot woven by Nogaret went back to 1303. That
year, a Templar, a native of Beziers and a high official
of the Order, had been deprived of his post for a personal crime, and then, having failed to obtain another
from the provincial governor of Mont-Carmel, he had
assassinated this governor in his residence near Milan.
He had then escaped to Paris and had been received
by Nogaret, to whom he revealed the so-called abomina-
tions practiced by the Templars. Nogaret immediately

realized the part which this wretch, Esquiu de Floryan, could be made to play, for Esquiu boasted that he knew the secrets of the Order. Nogaret imprisoned him in the royal chateau of Toulouse and gave him as his cell companion a man condemned to death for murder. The two men confided in one another, and the murderer, terrified by what he heard, sought and obtained an audience with the king. As a result of these "revelations" Philip the Fair, who had previously been withheld by certain doubts and scruples, immediately proclaimed to the Christian world the iniquities of the Templars. By way of precaution, Philip sent Esquiu de Floryan to Lerida to impart the same information to James II of Aragon, so that he might obtain support from the Spanish king.

In 1305, at the death of Benedict XI, the short-lived successor of Boniface VIII, the election of Bertrand de Got gave an impetus to the plans of Philip and Nogaret. A secret interview took place between the Archbishop of Bordeaux and the king, during which the king promised Bertrand that he would secure the Tiara for him on certain conditions, the final condition not to be revealed to the new Pope until after his election. This final condition was the support of the Holy See towards the suppression of the Templars.[2]

Clement V was not capable of open resistance to a man like Philip whom he feared as ardently as he secretly detested. The Pope vacillated and constantly postponed decision, but at length he summoned James de Molay to France to defend the Templars against certain accusations. The Grand Master left Cyprus, where the Order had its headquarters, and came to

France. The Grand Master of the Knights Hospitallers, summoned at the same time, refused to come.

James de Molay went first to Poitiers where Clement V then held his court. King Philip was also at Poitiers, and he received the Grand Master with a display of honor and attention, for he hoped to find him an invaluable tool for his purposes. Philip's original intention was to make the Order an instrument of his policy and to secure that the Grand Mastership should devolve upon his son and should become an hereditary post in the royal House of France. This was too much for James de Molay. Meantime, Nogaret was continuing to weave his plots in secret, but nothing could be accomplished without the support of the Pope. On September 13, 1307, the king decided on his grand coup. He conferred with his habitual councillors, Nogaret and the Grand Inquisitor of France. An order was issued to all those whom it concerned to proceed to the arrest of the Templars throughout the entire Kingdom. The coup was particularly successful because the secret had been rigorously kept until the last moment to secure the effect of surprise. In Paris, Nogaret personally directed the operation.

The Pope's reaction to the news was one of intense indignation. He suspended the powers of the ecclesiastical judges and even of the Inquisitors. Philip, in extreme irritation, sent to him a carefully chosen group of prisoners, but not the most important dignitaries of the Order. They were received in Poitiers by Cardinals Beranger Fredol and Etienne de Suisy, both creatures of the French king, and they repeated in the Papal presence the admissions which had been extracted from them under torture. The Pope immediately gave in, restored their powers to the ordinary judges, reserved to himself in due course the examination of the higher dignitaries, and, in the Bull *Pastoralis Praeeminentiae,* directed Christian princes to arrest the Templars and confiscate their property.

The king's agents behaved with unspeakable brutality towards the prisoners. The Inquisitors, in the circumstances, put themselves at the disposal of the civil power. James de Molay and Hugh de Pairaud, visitor of France, were not spared. Under torture, they made confessions which they were later to retract. The whole business was a monument of iniquity. Nothing was spared to extract confessions from the Templars of crimes which they had never committed, as was proved among other things by the fact that one "confession" contradicted another made by the same man. They were made to admit that, on admission to the Order, they had to walk on and spit at (or "near") the Crucifix. Unnatural vice was one of the accusations against them. The idol Baphomet—a corruption of the name Mahomet—existed only in the overheated brains of the torturers. But, in the grip of pain, the unfortunate men, some of them old and already debilitated by the climate of the East, admitted anything put to them. The speech of one of the Knights to the papal commissioners stands out, in which he says: "Because of the torturers ... I would, I think, admit anything. I would admit that I killed God if I were asked to admit it." A considerable number of the Knights died in their cells as a result of the tortures they had undergone; others gave in when they were about to be subjected to further torture.

It was not merely greed for the property of the Knights that actuated Philip the Fair. He was obsessed with the desire to find out their so-called "secret" and to discover the hidden aims of the Order. He failed to do so. If this secret existed, it was not revealed by those who knew it. The admissions extracted from others were useless, since they came from those who would not have been among "the initiated," anyhow, if such existed at all.

The Pope again sought to reserve the whole affair to himself. The Order could have been saved, but Philip reacted with lightning rapidity. He obtained the approbation of the *Faculte de theologie* of Paris for the measures he had taken, and then he summoned the State Assembly to meet in Tours at Easter 1308. The assembly declared the Templars worthy of death and petitioned the king to extirpate their pernicious heresy. After that, the king went to Poitiers, knelt at the Pope's feet, but refused to mitigate his severity towards the Templars.

Philip, rather than give in to the Pope on this vital point, even threatened him to such an extent that Clement attempted unsuccessfully to escape from Poitiers. Having again caused a carefully chosen group of seventy-two Templars to "confess" in the Pope's presence, the king finally obtained a Bull addressed to the French hierarchy by which the suspensions were lifted. The trials could begin again, not only in France but wherever the Templars had establishments.

In Paris, a pontifical commission had been constituted before whom James de Molay appeared on November 26, 1309. The Grand Master retracted the pseudo-confessions he had made under torture. He deliberately took up the defense of his Order with a rough candor that alienated his judges. Philip the Fair had appointed his faithful counsellor, William of Plaisans, to attend the interrogations.

But the moment of decision had yet to come. Clement V had undertaken to commit the affair of the Templars to an Ecumenical Council. This council assembled at Vienna in October 1311, and Philip was in attendance. It dragged on for several months, and it was only in April 1312, by the Bull *Considerantes dudum* approved by the Fathers of the Council, that the Order was suppressed without the Knights having been given the chance to present their case for the defense. Portugal alone refused to ratify the conciliar decrees, and the remnant of the Templars reconstituted themselves there under a new name, the Order of Christ. Henry the Navigator used them to organize those voyages of discovery to which he owes his name.

Meantime, James de Molay was in prison. The Pope named a commission to hear his case and to reach a final verdict. On March 19, 1314, Molay and the master of Normandy, his colleague, having been pronounced guilty on their own previous admissions, were brought before the main entrance of Notre Dame to be publicly sentenced to life imprisonment. To save their lives, they only needed to remain silent, but the whole business took an unexpected turn. Molay made a sign that he wished to speak. He expressed his sorrow, not as was expected for his crimes, but for having, through the false confessions extorted from him under torture, betrayed and calumniated a pure and holy Order. "The Order is holy and without stain.

The accusations are ridiculous, and our confessions a tissue of lies." His companion, Charnay, associated himself with this declaration, and thereby they both put themselves in the category of the relapsed. The ecclesiastical judges had no other course than to put them again in the charge of the Governor of Paris, not to execute them, but to allow time for overnight deliberation. But Philip, in extreme rage at this turn of events, acted immediately. The two Knights were rushed to the stake and given to the flames that same evening. They both went to their death with courage and serenity. There is a tradition that, when the flames began to lick his feet, Molay spoke aloud his indignation and summoned Clement V and Philip the Fair to appear soon before the Tribunal of God. However this may be, they both did die in that same year 1314.

In the tragic affair of the Templars, we have a pattern which recurs several times in later history—the clear domination of the civil power over the ecclesiastical power. If Clement V had been a man of greater energy and had not been practically at the mercy of the French king—or, in other words, if the Templars had been able to stand trial for alleged heresy before pontifical judges—the outcome would have been completely different. Unfortunately, the Grand Inquisitor of France, William Imbert of Paris, confessor of Philip the Fair, and the other members of the tribunal who in theory should have been dependent only on the Holy See, allowed themselves in practice to be made the cat's paws of the royal authority to such an extent that, as we have seen, the Pope was twice led to suspend their powers.

Here we have a typical example of the force used against the judges and of the unwarranted meddling of the civil authority in something appertaining to the ecclesiastical forum. To a great extent, the case against the Templars was conducted with revolting partiality and, unfortunately, with the complicity of the Pontifical Inquisition.

---

1. The reader may be referred to Funck-Brentano: Le Moyen Age (English translation: Heinemann, London); Michelet: Proces de Templiers (2 vols.) which gives the original minutes of the trial; and Addison: The Knights Templars, valuable for the account it gives of the suppression of the Order in England. (Translators notes)

2. This is disputed. See the reference to Hefele-Leclerq in Hughes: History of the Church, Vol. 3 p. 90, footnote.

CHAPTER SIX

The Inquisition and the Heresy
of the Spirituals

The history of the Protestant Reformation in the
sixteenth century is fully intelligible only if we study
its origins in the many heterodox currents which under-
lay the apparently undisturbed religious unity of the
Middle Ages. There are various explanations for this
multiplicity of heresies. Such proliferation was, no
doubt, increased by reaction against the splendor and
extravagance and often the lax behavior of the higher
clergy. The ignorance of the lower clergy, which
reached scandalous proportions in certain countries,
left them deplorably inadequate to refute men whose
mode of life was clearly more holy than theirs and who
had a knowledge of Scripture which they utterly
lacked. In addition, there was a thirst for the miracu-
lous and the wonderful in a society as yet little developed, and among certain people a tendency towards
mystical enthusiasm which on the one hand, led to

the eminent sanctity of a Saint Francis, a Saint Bona-
venture, and later a Catherine and a Bernardine of
Siena, while it also resulted, on the other hand, in
aberrations directly leading to heresy, from the theological viewpoint, and to anarchy or something similar
in the social domain.

In these conditions, we can better understand the
complexity of the Church's task to maintain the integrity of revealed truth and to separate the grain
from the chaff. Here the role of the Inquisition can be
more clearly seen and justified than in those circumstances where the civil power seized upon it for its
own purposes. Now, one of the characteristics of the
struggle against heresy in the fourteenth and fifteenth
centuries is highly interesting. We frequently find
Franciscan Inquisitors acting against fellow-Francis-
cans who were guilty of pushing beyond reasonable
limits the logical deductions from the ideal conceived
and taught by Saint Francis. This was the case, not
only in France, but in Italy, Germany, Flanders, Poland, England, and Spain prior to the institution there
of the Spanish Inquisition which we shall study in a
later chapter.

Quite clearly, the strictly literal observance of the
Franciscan rule about poverty was practically incompatible with the very irradiation and apostolic activity
of the Friars Minor. Although the Religious needed to
possess nothing as individually owned, they nevertheless needed houses to live in and the necessaries to
furnish food and clothing. In the thirteenth century,
the very idea of an Order founded on the principle
of poverty was a novel one, not without its savor of
paradox. There were, of course, monks who made a per-

sonal vow of poverty, but they belonged to an abbey or monastery which held considerable property and whose abbot maintained the splendor of a great feudal lord. The mendicants of Saint Dominic and Saint Francis were not monks, since the latter word implies the idea of stability through attachment to a particular monastery.

The appearance of the Mendicant Orders more or less coincided with the break up of the feudal system and the emergence of the Communes organized on a democratic basis. It has often been remarked that a distinct parallel exists between the internal structure of a Religious Order or Congregation and that of the contemporary civil society. Thus, the Benedictine Order and its collateral branches correspond in pattern to the feudal world; the Mendicants are modeled on the medieval Communes; and later, the Counter-Reformation Jesuits and other Congregations founded in the second half of the sixteenth century, are organized on the model of absolute monarchy.

Let us return, however, to the Franciscans. Saint Francis' successor, Brother Elias of Cortona, a man of strong and realistic views as well as being the distinguished architect of the Basilica of Assisi, sought and obtained from the Holy See considerable modifications to the rule and to the system of absolute poverty. Many of the spiritual sons of Saint Francis who had abandoned all they possessed to celebrate their mystical marriage to Lady Poverty, were offended by these modifications, and they sought to uphold what had been the ideal of the seraphic Father. Medieval society of the thirteenth and fourteenth century had dealt a blow to that ideal. To catch the quality of its fervor, however, one need only read the incomparable Canto XII of Dante's *Paradiso*. Thus, from its very outset, a twofold current developed in the Franciscan movement. This must be kept clearly in mind if we are to understand how one current, that of "the Spirituals," went astray into heresy, and how the Inquisition had then to intervene to combat and suppress it.

Brother Elias, several times deposed and re-elected as General of the Order, was opposed by the survivors of the first Franciscan generation, among them the famous Brother Leo whom Francis used to call "God's little sheep." When Elias of Cortona was constructing the Basilica, he had placed in the nave a marble box for offerings. Moved with holy indignation, Brother Leo smashed this box, an action which caused him to be exiled to a Friary far from Assisi.

After the apprehensions which preceded the year 1000 A.D., medieval society of the eleventh, twelfth and even thirteenth centuries manifested a new form of unrest. A new era was felt to be at hand, and almost everywhere among the lower ranks of society there was rebellion against the wealthy higher clergy and against priests with wives or concubines—a rebellion which even led people to refuse the Sacraments if they were administered by unworthy priests. Certain places, Milan and Lombardy in particular, were the seed-beds of this attitude which could in the long run degenerate into open revolution. At first, the Holy See tended rather to encourage this popular aggression against lax and licentious clergy.

The day was to come, however, when the legitimate authority of the Church itself would be threatened by the ever increasing tendency to substitute for the sacerdotal ministry the apostolate of a laity without mandate. Under pretence of returning to primitive Christianity, laymen were preaching in public places, administering Baptism, and dissuading the faithful from turning to their priests even at the hour of death. Even before the time of Saint Francis, a violent dispute was in existence between the monks and the secular clergy.

With the rapid growth of the Franciscan movement and the multiplication of religious walking barefooted from place to place, preaching in the open, and practicing absolute poverty, this hostility between the seculars and the regulars could not fail to increase. Undoubtedly, the sons of Saint Francis were carrying out a highly praiseworthy task and doing immense good in the heart of a society in full change. But some of them evinced a religious and mystical exaltation which would, sooner or later, lead them into a dangerous path. Furthermore certain eccentric ideas already in circulation were betraying simple minds into extreme and dangerous attitudes.

The Apocalypse has always more or less served as a source book for the prophetic utterances of those who believe in the imminence of the Second Coming and of the Last Judgment. Something of the kind marks the period we are dealing with. One of the sources to which minds in quest of prophetic exaltation turned at that time was the famous work, *The Eternal Gospel* of Joachim of Flora (or Fiori: C. 1135-1202). This strange and attractive twelfth century mystic was to have a profound influence on many of the Franciscans. Son of a notary of Celico in Calabria, Joachim spent some time as a young man in Palermo at the court of Roger II of Sicily.

The king, of Norman blood, lived a life of wholly oriental luxury, surrounded by Jews, Arabs and numerous concubines, as well as monks and prelates, minstrels and other entertainers. Despite his good looks, Joachim came through uncorrupted. Roger, who regarded him highly, sent him on a diplomatic mission to Constantinople, accompanied by a kind of Palmeritan hermit. They reached the shores of the Bosphorus at a time when the imperial city was being ravaged by a frightful plague. The horror of it all made a deep impression on Joachim, and in reaction against the luxury of Palermo, he resolved to make a pilgrimage with his companion to the Holy Land. This meant an extremely long and painful journey across the Syrian desert, at the end of which he arrived exhausted in Jerusalem and remained there for a year.

Seized with enthusiastic fervor, convinced that he had been given a divine mission, Joachim then set off for Calabria, and on his way passed through Palermo where in the meantime Roger II had died. Having overcome his father's opposition, he was admitted as a lay Brother into a monastery of Cistercians. His superiors ordered him to study for the priesthood, and in due course he was elected Abbot of Corazzo. With the passage of time Joachim gained a high reputation for holiness and the gift of prophecy. He then obtained the Pope's permission to retire with some of his Religious to the Sila (a woody Calabrian plateau) where he founded a community of hermits at San Giovanni in Fiore, whence their name "the Florensian Order." Through contemplating the miseries attendant on the quarrels over investiture, Joachim came to formulate his doctrine of the three successive ages: the age of the Father, the Period covered by the Old Testament; the age of the Son, from the birth of Christ to about 1260; the age of the Holy Ghost from that date onwards. This last would be a reign of purity within the framework of a new society in which the monks would be the spiritual rulers and guides.

Our concern here is with the extent to which this Calabrian Abbot, placed by Dante in Paradise, exercised, through his *Eternal Gospel,* his concordances, his interpretations of the Apocalypse, his *Psalterium Decem Chordarum,* a profound influence on those Franciscans who, moved by an ever increasing desire for perfection, ended by falling into heresy and made it necessary for the Church to prosecute them, to summon them before the tribunal of the Inquisition and to pronounce their condemnation.

In his lifetime, long before the Inquisition, there were already those who regarded Joachim as holding extreme views verging on heresy. Joachim in answer to such criticism, voluntarily submitted his *Eternal Gospel*[1] and his other writings to the Holy See and the theological examiners then found nothing to censure in them. At a later examination, however, an error concerning the dogma of the Trinity was discovered, the Abbot having a tendency to a sort of tritheism. Joachim died in 1202 in the odor of sanctity.

Towards the middle of that admirable thirteenth century, so rich in intellectual ferment, the conflict had accentuated within the Franciscan Order between the advocates of mitigation and the Spirituals. The latter, intransigent on the question of absolute poverty, found the writings of the Calabrian Abbot to be a powerful support for their own ideas. His works, read, re-read and minutely studied, gave birth within the Order to Joachimist circles which so multiplied and increased in influence that, in the General Chapter at Avignon in 1247, Friar John of Parma was elected the new General. John of Parma, one of the most engaging figures of his day, belonged to the group of rigorists and ardently favored "the disciples of Joachim" within the Order. We know the severity of Pope Innocent IV towards heresy, and yet this Pope himself felt a very particular sympathy towards the Franciscan Spirituals. So matters continued until 1254, the year in which *The Eternal Gospel* was denounced by a group of Doctors of the University of Paris. They were concerned with the text edited by Gerard of Borgo San Donnino and preceded by an introduction in which Joachim's thesis about the passage from the Gospel of Christ to the Eternal Gospel was firmly stated.

The theories, whose advocates were religious of the Mendicant Orders, exasperated a certain group of University Doctors. Among them, the most militant was William of Saint-Amour, Canon of Beauvais. He published a book: *De Periculis Novissimorum Temporum* and thundered publicly against the new Orders, especially the Dominicans. The affair created a great stir, and William's book, denounced to the Holy See, was condemned at Anagni; but immediately afterwards, though with less noise, *The Eternal Gospel*, also submitted, was equally condemned.

It is useful to cover this ground. It shows that, in the midst of this age of Faith, there were other dangers besides the Cathari and the Waldenses. Even within a

Religious Order founded by Saint Francis for the purpose of a radical reform of the Church, we find groups who will soon detach themselves, like dead branches, from the living tree of the authentic Franciscan family, to create dangerous disorders everywhere and thereby compel the Church to act against them.

The upholders of the principle of absolute poverty among the Franciscans were eventually known in Italy as the *Fraticelli* and in France as the *Fraticelles*. They were numerous in Lyons but at first they restrained themselves within certain limits. An unexpected event, however, led to the lifting of all restraint. The death of Pope Nicholas IV in 1292 was followed by an interminable conclave prolonged for close on two years, such was the disorder reigning in the Italian peninsula and so violent the conflicts between opposing factions.

In the end, the King of Naples, Charles II of Anjou, brought his influence to bear on the eleven Cardinals who could not agree, and a unanimous choice was made of an old man of seventy, Peter of Murrone, who had been living for many years as a hermit in the remote solitudes of the Abruzzi. He was enthroned as Pope at Aquila, and took the name Celestine V. His entire reign comes within the year 1294: July 5, his election; August 29, his enthronement; December 13, his resignation-the "great refusal"—for which Dante placed him in Hell, but which did not prevent the Church from canonizing him. During his brief Pontificate, groups of the Fraticelli came to Celestine—a man of immense holiness but also, as one contemporary puts it, of "entire and dangerous simplicity"—and persuaded him to reverse the policy of his predecessors by authorizing them to practice the Rule of Saint Francis in all its primitive strictness. Celestine knew two of the Spirituals, Peter of Maurata and Peter of Fossombrone, both of whom he held in high regard. It was they whom he released from obedience to their Superiors, and authorized to live as hermits in a condition of absolute poverty.

The outcome was short-lived. After Celestine's abdication, his successor, Boniface VIII, formerly the energetic Cardinal Caetani, revoked the decree and began again the prosecutions against the Spirituals. The hermits grouped around Peter of Fossombrone, who had changed his name to Brother Angelo Clareno, declared that they did not recognize the abdication of Pope Celestine and refused to submit. Their leader was the learned, charming and austere young Brother Peter John Olivi, whose doctrine was tinged with modified Joachimism. Olivi died in 1298, and afterwards the Fraticelli multiplied, especially since they were joined by many laymen of the Franciscan Third Order who took the name of Beguins or Beguines.

Under successive Pontificates, Boniface VIII, Clement V and John XXII strove to suppress such groups who were adopting an increasingly hostile attitude to the Church, to its riches, to its authority, and becoming less and less distinguishable from the Waldensian heretics. After Olivi's death, the Spirituals were led by a Franciscan of Narbonne, Bernard Delicieux, and by Ubertino de Casale whose writings were a continuation of those of Olivi. The influence of the Fraticelli could not fail to increase in the South-West of France in particular, where it led to the expulsion from their Friaries of the Franciscans who were opposed to the principle of absolute poverty.

Our account has brought us to the year 1317, when,

faced with their obstinacy, Pope John XXII instructed the Inquisitors at Languedoc to treat the Fraticelli and the Beguins as heretics. The conflict began. At the end of the same year, the Pope issued a Bull of excommunication against the sect in France, and, some weeks later, steps of an identical kind were taken against the Tuscan Spirituals led by Enrico de Ceva. On April 27, 1318, a certain number of the Friars Minor of Narbonne and of Beziers, with Bernard Delicieux as their leader, were made to appear before the Cardinals assembled at the Pontifical Palace of Avignon, the Pope himself presiding. Called upon to submit, forty did so, the other twenty five remained obdurate.

The Inquisitor of Provence and Forcalquier, Michel le Moine, himself a Franciscan, took the rebels in charge, and, at the conclusion of their trial, delivered four of them to the secular arm. They were given to the flames at Marseilles. One other was condemned to life imprisonment, and the rest incurred only light sentences. Bernard Delicieux was condemned to life imprisonment. Besides the accusations of a doctrinal nature brought against him, he was also arraigned for having provoked public disorder and for having incited the people of Carcassonne against the Inquisitors.

Here we are concerned with questions which are, in a sense, much more complicated than those concerning the Cathari, the Waldenses, and other professed and dangerous heretics, whose doctrines, especially those of the Cathari, attacked the very foundations of society. The Fraticelli were Religious more or less lacking in discipline; the Beguins were tertiaries affiliated to a great Order. Their rigorism had been approved to some extent and generally encouraged by the Popes prior to John XXII, not only by Celestine V but by Nicholas III and even, up to a certain point, by Boniface VIII and Clement V.

The upholders of the theories prosecuted by the Inquisition made such frequent and such effective appeal to pontifical texts, in their defense, that the Avignon Pope, wishing to end the whole matter, appointed a commission of theologians charged with pronouncing a definitive sentence. This was no easy task in view of the fact that, in the meantime, the General Chapter of the Order, presided over by Michael of Cesena who was influenced by the celebrated William of Ockham and by Friar Buonagrazia of Verona, once more accepted as well founded the theses held by the Spirituals. Nevertheless, in the Bull *Cum Inter Nonnullos* (November 12, 1323), John XXII solemnly condemned the tenets of the Spirituals and of the Fraticelli.

The obstinacy of the Fraticelli in not submitting to the decisions of the Holy See was partly explained by their having found a protector in the person of Emperor Louis of Bavaria. At the death of Henry VII of Luxemburg, the sovereign in whom Dante had rested high hopes, cut short by the premature end of the Germanic Caesar, the imperial crown had been simultaneously attributed to Frederick of Austria and Louis of Bavaria. The Pope attempted to settle the dispute by seeking to impose a third candidate of his own choice, the leader of the Italian Guelph party, Robert of Anjou, king of Naples. Meantime, the struggle between the two Germans continued, and Louis of Bavaria succeeded in capturing his opponent. For all that, he did not succeed in obtaining recognition by the Holy

See. John XXII summoned him, under pain of excommunication to Avignon. The Emperor continued
to ignore this summons and was finally excommunicated
in 1334. This almost coincided with the excommunication of the Spirituals, a fact which led the estranged
Franciscans and the Emperor to make common cause.
In a solemn declaration, the Emperor denounced the
misbehavior of John XXII and espoused the cause of
the Spirituals, the supposedly true disciples of that
Saint Francis to whom God had revealed the primitive
Rule and confirmed that Rule by witness of the Stig-
mata.

The Pope reacted vigorously. He ordered the Bishops of Germany to arrest and to send him any Religious
suspected of having been involved in the drawing up
of the imperial declaration and of upholding the duly
condemned doctrine of absolute poverty. This already
tense situation was further envenomed by the fact that
the General of the Order, Michael of Cesena, seemed
vexatiously reticent about the Papal decisions and
condemnations. He was summoned to Avignon, where
John XXII ordered both him and Friar Buonagrazia
of Bergamo to remain. Fearing that they would fall
into the hands of the Inquisition, the two Religious
fled by night and succeeded in escaping to Italy. The
Pope immediately deposed Michael from his General-
ship, charged him with heresy, and ordered the Inquisitor of Provence to act against him. Michael reached
the court of Louis of Bavaria at Pisa. He sided with
the ephemeral anti-Pope, Nicholas V, created by the
Emperor, and he died, still estranged, in 1348. Louis
of Bavaria had died the year before.

John XXII, who had become Pope at the age of

seventy-two—twenty seven months after the death of
Clement V—was the victim of calumniators who accused him, not only of practicing nepotism excessively,
but also of accumulating riches to a scandalous extent.
The reality was quite otherwise. John XXII, who led
an austere and mortified life, had found at his election
that the finances of the Church were in a deplorable
condition. He proved such an incomparable admini-
strator that at the end of his eighteen years reign, he
left the finances of the Church in a very healthy state.
Perhaps John XXII owed to his outstanding administra-
tive and legal cast of mind, the love he professed for
clear and well defined situations.

The more or less cloudy theories of the Spirituals,
the apocalyptic visions borrowed from Joachim of Flora,
made him shudder. Much more energetic than his
predecessor, Clement V, he relied much more on the
Inquisition. During his reign, the pontifical tribunal
was in constant session. In the South of France, where
the sect of the Fraticelli had multiplied, the Bishop of
Elne, Beranger Batte, was directed to carry out an
inquiry into the doctrine of the absolute poverty of
Christ and His Apostles, preached and taught by the
Franciscan, William Negre. The threat of being handed
over to the Inquisition caused a considerable number
of Fraticelli and of the Beguins to attempt an escape
to Greece and Palestine, and funds were collected by
one of their adherents, Pierre Trencavel, who ended
by being arrested at Carcassonne, imprisoned, re-imprisoned after escape, and handed over to Jean Dupont,
the Grand Inquisitor of Carcassone. With a certain
number of his companions, among them two priests,
he was condemned to life imprisonment.

Sometimes the heretics sought sanctuary in churches or convents. At the request of King Philip VI of Valois, John XXII authorized the agents of the secular power to seize them wherever found, in exchange for which concession the king allowed the Inquisitors to prosecute the adherents of Louis of Bavaria who had come in great numbers from Italy into France. The Pope's zeal in the pursuit of heresy did not relent, and it extended even to the diocese of Paris where a number of the Fraticelli were in hiding. At the Pope's request, the king facilitated the prosecution which a Canon of Notre Dame was charged to bring against Cecco d'Ascoli, abettor of the anti-Pope.

The Bishop of Paris himself, Hugues-Michel of Besancon, and the Doctors of the University, showed great zeal against the heretics and especially against a certain Geraldo Rostagno of Genoa, accused of having assisted the flight from Avignon of Michael of Cesena, General of the Franciscans. In 1330, another of the Fraticelli was brought before the Inquisition. This was a certain Conrad, who had openly accused Pope John XXII of holding an heretical doctrine about the condition of the souls of the dead prior to the Last Judgment. The Grand Inquisitor of France, Aubert Chalons, assisted by the Bishop of Paris, conducted the case. However, through the intervention of Queen Jeanne of France, the accused was set free, and the Pope was satisfied with his repentance. In other places, notably in Majorca and in the Province of Roussillon, the Inquisition had to occupy itself with the Fraticelli and the Beguins.

In Italy, and especially in the Kingdom of Naples, the successor of Michael of Cesena instituted proceedings against two Spirituals. King Robert of Anjou, urged by his wife, Queen Sanche, attempted to hinder the action of the tribunal, but John XXII vigorously intervened and charged the Queen with supporting the Fraticelli.

In Germany, on account of the conflict between the Pope and Louis of Bavaria, the situation took a more serious turn than elsewhere. The Emperor's support had enabled the Spirituals, now become enemies of the Papacy, to assume a rapidly increasing importance. In regions not subject to Louis of Bavaria, where its action was not hindered by the imperial authority, the Inquisition had much ado to detect the heretics and to put an end to their activities.

Already, in the Rhineland, a mystical current had established itself, represented among others by Master Eckhart, a Dominican who died in 1327. From Eckhart's writings, Pope John XXII had extracted a certain number of propositions which were judged to be erroneous and dangerous. There existed in the Rhineland an atmosphere of "enthusiasm," a climate of exalted ideas, favorable to the diffusion of heretical sects. One such sect took its name from a Dutchman, Lollard Walter, who preached a doctrine whose essential elements adumbrated the errors of Wyclif, John Huss, and Luther. His followers, the Lollards, took on a certain importance. The founder of the sect was arrested and died at the stake, having refused to retract or to denounce his followers. Meantime, in Germany and in the diocese of Cologne, many groups of Beguins were discovered, and some fifty of their number were burnt alive. The Archbishop of Cologne and the other bishops of the region, including the Bishop of Metz, personally directed the repression of heresy, with the result that it is with the episcopal rather than with the Pontifical Inquisition that one is dealing here.

However, in view of the seriousness of the situation, the Rhine bishops felt the need for coordination. In 1340, it was an Augustinian called Jordan who presided in Saxony, under the authority of the bishops. Later, in the reign of Charles IV of Luxemburg, successor to Louis of Bavaria and entirely devoted to the Holy See, the Inquisition became directly dependent on the Pope, and a Dominican, John Schlandelang of Strasbourg, was appointed Grand Inquisitor for the whole of Germany.

During the second half of the fourteenth century, the Inquisition was kept particularly busy by having to deal with a new peril. In the aftermath of the frightful Black Death, there were manifestations in Germany of decidedly anarchic mysticism. The already existing sects, Fraticelli, Beguins, Lollards, came together to join forces with those now notorious "flagellants" who, urged on by the Spirituals, went through towns and countryside scourging their naked torsos to blood and provoking scenes of hysteria rather than of true piety. Pope Clement VI, successor to John XXII, severely condemned all this, and the Inquisition had to intervene.

Under the succeeding Pontificates of Innocent VI and Urban V, the inquisitorial powers of the Dominicans were renewed by the Holy See in the province of Mayence, the dioceses of Basle and Strasbourg and the Archdiocese of Besancon. The Emperor Charles IV restored to their full vigor the edicts against heretics promulgated more than a century earlier by Frederick

II of Hohenstaufen, and gave the unlimited support
of the secular arm to the Dominican Inquisitors ,notably
to Ludwig von Caliga and Walter Kellinger, promoted
to their posts by Urban V.

It might seem at first sight that the Great Schism
would have diminished the activity of the Inquisition,
but the opposite happened. The division of the Church
into two rival obediences gradually created such excessive disorder, especially in Germany, that the Inquisitors were fully engaged in prosecuting the different sects, now more active and more numerous than
ever in the Germanic regions. In the two years, 1394
and 1395, the Provincial of the Celestines succeeded,
without recourse to cruelty, in reconciling a great
number of heretics to the Church. The movement of
the Spirituals had taken on at first a mystical and
speculative character.

The English Franciscan, William of Ockham, for
some years a Professor of the University of Paris and
one of the major figures in the famous quarrel about
universals, was exclusively theoretic. His doctrines
were to contribute in some measure towards misleading
Luther and Calvin in the sixteenth century. William
went to the court of Louis of Bavaria and there met
and made common cause with imperial legists such
as Marsilius of Padua and John of Jandun, implacable
enemies of the temporal claims of the Holy See. Gradually, however, the theories of the Spirituals grew to
have more and more popular appeal, with social consequences leading to a kind of dangerous communism.

This was what happened in England under the
inspiration of John Wyclif, a secular priest and Oxford
Professor, a real precursor, not only of John Huss, but

of the Anglican schism and of the Protestant Reformation. Wyclif was a bitter enemy of the Papacy, but constant Royal protection thwarted the attempts made by the Holy See to bring him before the Inquisition. Full of riches and honors, he died in 1384, in his parish of Lutterworth, without having been reconciled with the Church. At the Council of Constance, a theologian was able to present one hundred and sixty manifestly heretical propositions extracted from the works of Wyclif. Their special character was that they entailed consequences calculated to overthrow the social order. According to Wyclif, only a person in the state of grace had the power to exercise a public function, including kingship, or even to hold property. Since the state of grace is something impossible to pronounce upon in any individual case, it is apparent that anarchy lay in such a proposition. Wyclif also rejected the idea of the *patria,* the fatherland, in the sense that he ruled it out by proclaiming an attitude of absolute non-resistance to the aggressor. The lucubrations of this English contemporary of Chaucer contain ideas we were to meet again in Tolstoy.

Wyclif's doctrines soon bore fruit. Under their inspiration, many Lollards banded together to impose their ideas in the North of England and even in London where, in 1381 on the Feast of Corpus Christi, they assassinated the Archbishop of Canterbury. However, Wyclifism was to have even more serious consequences in Bohemia, where John Huss, an avowed disciple of the Oxford Professor condemned by the Council of Constance, was to unleash civil war in the name of principles identical with those of Wyclif. This identity emerges clearly in the Council's condemnation of the following Hussite doctrine: "Any man in a state of sin is not temporal prince or prelate or bishop." John Huss and his disciple, Jerome of Prague, presented themselves before the Council of Constance, provided with a safe conduct from the Emperor Sigismond.

Relying on this imperial protection, Huss preached publicly, refused to recognize that he was excommunicated, said Mass openly, and opposed the Council Fathers so obstinately that they refused to admit that such an averred heretic should be able to come and go as he pleased. Imprisoned after having refused to retract except on some points of detail, John Huss and Jerome of Prague were condemned by an ecclesiastical tribunal, handed over to the secular arm, and burned alive at Constance on July 6, 1415. It is notable that John Huss was condemned as an heresiarch adherent of the theories of Wyclif.

Much has been written and there have been heated controversies about the trial and (no doubt courageous) death of these two men. One can deal fairly with the matter only by constantly reminding oneself of the age in which it happened—an age when the very idea of tolerance was unknown. Of course, one shudders in horror at the idea of a man being burnt to death for his ideas, however erroneous; but, on the other hand, it is impossible to deny the evil and the disturbances caused by the diffusion of these ideas, especially among the easily led masses.

In this connection, one has only to remember the inexorable Hussite wars which ravaged Bohemia throughout a great part of the fifteenth century. The disciples of the heresiarch took refuge on a mountain which they fortified and named Mount Thabor, whence they were called Thaborites. They spread into the whole country, sacking churches, convents and princely residences. Priests, merchants, townsfolk, who fell into their hands, were mercilessly butchered. In such conditions, the Church could not but take measures, for they were such as gave full justification to the Inquisition. To meet this widespread and long continuing scourge, Pope Nicholas V conferred the title of Grand Inquisitor for the whole of Europe on a Franciscan who was later canonized as Saint John Capistran. The work of this celebrated preacher was to complete that of Saint Bernardine of Siena. The Pope sent him to Bohemia. He also sent Aeneas Sylvius Piccolomini—the future Pope Pius II—and the celebrated Cardinal Nicholas of Cusa.

Saint John Capistran is the model Inquisitor, enemy of brute force and firmly opposed to the use of torture. His great means was preaching, and he did not shirk public debates with heretics. He pardoned all who repented, and arrested only those whose crimes were notorious and inexpiable. He handed over to the secular arm only those who, having repented once, relapsed into their errors and committed one of the crimes severely punishable by civil law.

His greatest concern was with equity and justice. Hence he showed much more severity towards the powerful and the rich, whose responsibility was heavier, than towards the poor and the obscure whose simplicity and ignorance could have led them into error. His work carried him to many countries. In Tuscany, he fought energetically against the groups of the Spirituals who, on the model of what had occurred or was still occurring in Germany and England, were creating a climate of anarchy and of social disturbance.

At the end of the thirteenth century and the beginning of the fourteenth, the sect of the Apostolic Brethren, founded at Parma by a certain Gerard Segerelli, had made considerable progress in the Emilia-Romagna region and in the Marches. Then had arisen the famous Fra Dolcino, son of a priest of Vercelli, professing a very confused doctrine, a mixture of Manicheism and Catharism. To the principle of absolute poverty, he added that of free union, and he went around escorted by a woman "companion." Four crusades, directed by the Bishop of Vercelli, were required to defeat the little army of the heresiarch, who had entrenched himself in the neighboring mountains. Brought before an ecclesiastical tribunal, he refused to retract, and was burned alive on the banks of the river Sesia, in 1307. The influence of the Dolcinists and of the Spirituals generally was still felt a century and a half later, and it was thus that Saint John Capistran was led to combat the Fraticelli in Tuscany. Again, in the kingdom of Naples, Queen Joanna charged the Grand Inquisitor to act against the many Jews who were practicing usury.

Finally, his duties carried John Capistran as far as Poland where, by his zeal and eloquence he converted and baptized many Jews, not without thereby incurring implacable hatred.

---

1. This title was, in fact, not given to the work by Joachim of Flora. It was added by the Franciscan, Gerard da Borgo San Donnino, author of Liber Introductorius in Evangelium Aeternum, the latter being an edited and somewhat modified collection of Joachim's writings. The Liber was published long after Joachim's death.

CHAPTER SEVEN

Interference of the Civil Power With the Inquisition

The frightful tragedy of the Templars has already shown us the consequences that followed from excessive power exercised by the civil rulers over the ecclesiastical judges. This underlies the importance of drawing necessary distinctions if we are to gain a balanced idea of the Inquisition.

We meet an analogous case in the trial of Joan of Arc. If Pierre Cauchon, Bishop of Beauvais had not become the obedient servant of Henry VI, King of England, the Church of her own accord would never have brought a case against the Maid for heresy and sorcery, nor would she ever have made a martyr of the heroine of Domremy. The people themselves were not deceived, and, towards the end of the century, Francois Villon correctly interpreted their opinion when he spoke of "Joan, the good Joan, whom the English burned at Rouen." This also explains why, less than twenty five years after the Maid's death, the Holy Office, in 1456, under the Pontificate of the first Borgia Pope, Calixtus III, rehabilitated her, and why, centuries later, she was beatified by Pius X, canonized by Benedict XV, and created the second patron of France by Pius XI.

Our interest in Joan here is in the role played by the Inquisition during her trial, and we need not therefore deal with her life story. It was in March, 1430 that Joan, eight months after the consecration of Charles VII at Rheims, fell into the hands of the enemy before Compiegne in the course of a sortie aimed at delivering that town, then under siege by the Burgundian Jean de Luxembourg. The English archer who captured Joan sent her to Jean de Luxembourg, for she was a rich prize. She was taken to the chateau of Beaulieu in Vermandois. Knowing what awaited her and how merciless were her English enemies, after three months she attempted to escape—and not, as one historian little conversant with Catholic doctrine would have it, to commit suicide—by leaping from a seventy foot tower. She survived the fall and made no further attempt.

Jean de Luxembourg had no intention of yielding her up without a large ransom. During her stay at Beaulieu, she was in charge of the wife, aunt and sister-in-law of her captor, who treated her with high respect. Meantime, the hue and cry was raised by the University of Paris, whose Doctors, England dominated, looked upon Joan as a dangerous sorceress. They demanded that she should be handed over to

the Church and given to the Inquisition. According
to these Doctors, it was specifically to Pierre Cauchon,
Bishop of Beauvais, that she must be delivered, since
he had jurisdiction in Compiegne where she had been
captured. Cauchon, a man of devouring ambition and
known to detest Charles VII, was shamelessly in-
gratiating towards the English. He had installed himself
in Rouen in the hope of exchanging his modest diocese
for the rich Archbishopric of the Norman see. He directed the negotiations concerning Joan's ransom. The
English placed a heavy tax on Normandy, and gave
Jean de Luxembourg the sum of ten thousand gold
crowns to hand over the Maid to the Duke of Bur-
gundy. Meantime, Cauchon obtained from the Cathedral Chapter of Rouen an authorization to direct her
trial. She was transferred successively to Arras, Crotoy,
and then by various stages to Rouen at the end of
1430.

The trial began there on January 9, 1431. It com-
prised six public sessions and nine interrogations before
a more limited audience at the prison where Joan
was chained in a dark hole and closely guarded by
brutal soldiers. The spectacle is indeed heartrending of
this young girl, afflicted with physical suffering and
mental anguish, abandoned by all, even by her King
who did nothing to assist her. To sustain her, she had
only her "voices." She was faced with implacable judges,
armed with theology and syllogisms—certainly not intelligent, understanding men, but subtle and artful
foxes led by that frightful Cauchon whose ruthless
ambition left no place for compassion. Some among
them had fitful glimpses at times of the abominable

role they were being made to play and the iniquity
with which they were associated; but not so Pierre
Cauchon.

This infamous trial aptly illustrates and proves the
thesis we have been putting forward in this book. The
Inquisition was necessary to enable the Church to
defend her flock against the spread of error and against
the social evil engendered by perverse doctrines. But
the ecclesiastical court, episcopal or pontifical, with
all its imperfections consequent on the crudeness of
the age, pursued a purpose and accomplished a duty
in close connection with the supernatural mission of
the Church. On the other hand, however, abuses were
to be feared when the civil power dictated to the
ecclesiastical judges, in matters purely ecclesiastical,
the manner of conducting the trial and the verdict
to be reached. In the case of Joan of Arc, as in that
of the Templars, it was essential that the accused should
be condemned for having committed crimes contrary
to Christian morality. How could Joan possibly be
accused of such crimes? The English had met with
a series of reversals through this simple country girl.
She had declared that she had been sent by God to
drive them out of France, and that she was obeying
her "voices." Short of bowing to divine intervention,
the English and their allies had no alternative except
to impute to Joan the crime of sorcery or even of heresy
if she refused to recant. Michelet points out that her
judges were in a different position. "Among these Doctors," he writes, "were genuine theologians, sincere believers, men who had kept intact the firm faith of
the Middle Ages."

"It was not easy for such as these to reject apparitions and visions, for this would also be to throw doubt on all the wonders in the lives of the saints and to question all legends." Further on, he remarks: "It was indeed a strange sight to see these theologians, these doctors, using all their endeavors to destroy what was the basis of their doctrine and the religious principle of the Middle Ages in general—belief in revelations and the intervention of supernatural beings . . . . They perhaps had doubts about the angels, but their faith in the devil was firm and complete." We know in what spirit Michelet regarded the fundamental truths of Catholicism, but, in this particular instance, he put his finger on the evil. By conducting Joan's case as they did, Cauchon and his fellow fanatics were more than simply the docile instruments of a policy essentially opposed to the interests of France; they were also very bad servants of the Church, and, in the full sense of the word, advocates of the devil.

In their own way, the acts of the trial of Joan of Arc constitute one of the great monuments of French literature. Their value is all the greater for being due neither to style nor to literary polish. What constitutes their value are Joan's answers in which the flame of faith burns brightly to irradiate the whole text, and through which she effortlessly confounded her evil judges by clear good sense not unmixed, on occasion, with a telling flick of humor.

The accusations brought against Joan are such a hotchpotch of stupidity, lies and false pretexts, that they cover her judges with utter ridicule. The English alone had a vested interest in seeing that she was tried, judged, condemned and executed. In order to give an appearance of legality to this monstrous affair, Bedford, the representative of the young Henry VI, took every precaution that Joan should be tried by an ecclesiastical court. If she was to be condemned, it was necessary, they said, that she should be proved a witch and a heretic. Hence the emphasis by Cauchon on the fact that she wore men's clothes. To appreciate the import and the seriousness of this accusation, we must, of course, view it as Joan's age would have done. When Joan dressed like that, she was, as always, simply obeying her "voices," which had suggested this step to her as a commonsense precaution for consorting with soldiers. But we know what the judges made of this.

In prison, Joan was provided with woman's clothes which she put on. While she slept, however, her jailors removed them and left only her military gear. She had, of course, to put on—and then found herself *ipso facto* guilty of a relapse entailing condemnation to the stake! Like her Divine Master, Joan had to endure an ignominious death that she might enter into glory, but in her case it was not the counsel of the high priests who imposed their will on the representative of Caesar; it was the civil power which forced the Inquisition to ratify its will by pronouncing such a heinous sentence.

Twenty years later, this was exactly how Cardinal d'Estouteville saw the affair. Sent to France by Calixtus III to work for the reestablishment of peace between England and the Holy See, "he won distinction," says Pastor, "by introducing the process for the rehabilitation of Joan of Arc."

As we have seen, the fifteenth century was a period when sorcery, magic, witchcraft and superstition in various forms were a feature of social life, entailing the frequent intervention of the Inquisition. The sixteenth century was a much more advanced age in which we come face to face with what Lucien Febvre aptly calls "the problem of unbelief." The immense upheaveals consequent upon the Protestant Reformation, and the marvelous effort of re-orientation accomplished by the Catholic Reformation at Trent, modifies the viewpoint from which, up to this period, we have been studying the Inquisition. When, in Part Two of this book, we come to study the *Santa Hermandad* (the Spanish Inquisition), we shall examine its activity and the preponderant part it played in the struggle against the extension of northern Protestantism into the Iberian Peninsula and its overseas possessions.

As to the Pontifical Court, we shall content ourselves with briefly examining a few of its cases, especially in the eighteenth century, and we shall show that the picture, above all in Rome, is much less lurid than it is usually painted.

The period of heresies of the Manichean variety had passed. We are no longer concerned with this or that particular deviation, as we were in the twelfth, thirteenth and fourteenth centuries, in the case of, for example, Abelard, Berenger of Tours, or the Franciscan "Spirituals." The evil went deeper and affected the very sources of belief in God. If the sixteenth century was the age when everything was called in question, when the so-called reformers sought to lay the axe to the very trunk of the age-old tree which is the Church of Christ, the Council of Trent was at hand to restore order. After the furious tempest, Catholicism emerged diminished as to the number of its faithful but consolidated permanently on its foundations. From the second half of the sixteenth century, with the creation of new Religious Orders such as the Society of Jesus and many others, the Catholic renaissance is an astounding phenomenon.

In France under the influence among others of Saint Francis de Sales and Berulle, and in Rome under the influence of the Oratory of Saint Philip Neri, society was again becoming devout. But there was another side to the picture—a whole more or less camouflaged world was giving itself to real licentiousness of mind and manners. It was with the "libertines," which we must understand in the sense of "freethinkers," that the Inquisition was several times concerned. We shall consider four such cases—those of Giordano Bruno, Galileo, Tommaso Campanella, and Vannini. It is curious that two of these, Bruno and Campanella, were Dominicans.

The visitor to Rome will find in the Campo de'Fiori, a short distance from the Farnese Palace, a statue of Giordano Bruno in the Dominican habit. It was erected in 1889, through hatred of the Papacy, on the very spot where, on February 17, 1600, under the Pontificate of Clement VIII, this apostate philosopher, after a very long trial, was burned at the stake. The International Freethinkers Movement had made him one of its heroes and martyrs.

Giordano Bruno, a man of high intelligence and subtlety of mind, was born at Nola, near Naples, in

1548, and entered at a very early age the Neapolitan Friary of the Dominicans where Saint Thomas Aquinas had once resided. Of a restless mind and insatiably hungry for knowledge, he studied the philosophers of Antiquity, of the Middle Ages and of the Renaissance, and quickly developed a mortal hatred for Aristotelianism and for the Stagirite himself. He left the Dominicans and traveled successively in northern Italy, in France and Geneva. At Geneva, he adhered for a time to Calvinism, but soon attacked that position and was imprisoned. Released after retractation, he went on to Paris, where he won the protection of Henry III and became one of his *lecteurs;* thence to England, where Queen Elizabeth warmly welcomed him; then to Germany, and finally to Venice. There he came into the hands of the Inquisition.

In the course of his wanderings, Giordano Bruno had published many works, including numerous philosophical treatises, such as *De Umbris Idearum,* clearly pantheistic in content; *Spaccio della Bestia Trionfante* (dedicated to Sir Philip Sidney), the "triumphant beast" not being, as some have supposed, the Papacy, but Christianity as a whole including that of Luther and Calvin; *De Immenso, De Monade,* and *La Cena delle Ceneri,* and works on astronomy; and other works, including even a rather obscure comedy, *Il Candelaio,* published in Paris in 1582. A young patrician of Venice, Giovanni Mocenigo invited Giordano Bruno, then in Germany, to come and initiate him in the mnemotechnic science, the mysteries of which had been one of the preoccupations of Raymond Lulle in the thirteenth century. Whether because he found himself disillusioned or took fright at having received into his home a notorious heretic, the fact is that Mocenigo denounced Bruno to the Inquisition of Venice. The philosopher was arrested and cited before the Court. Bruno renounced all his previous opinions and promised to live henceforward as a good Christian. The noise of the affair had, however, reached Rome, and Clement VIII insisted that such a dangerous personage should be handed over for trial by the Inquisition of Rome. Giordano Bruno, it was urged, was merely a stranger in Venice, and the Pope, after much insistence, got his way.

Brought to Rome, Giordano Bruno spent six years there before being condemned to death. It is highly regrettable that the acts of his very long trial have never been discovered. Leo XIII, ever eager to throw the utmost possible light on the History of the Church, and, moreover, greatly incensed by the erection of the statue in the Campo de'Fiori, ordered the most minute search in the archives of the Holy Office for documents relative to the case, but all in vain. The French occupation at the time of the Directory, that of the imperial era, the Roman Republic of 1849, are no doubt sufficient explanation for their disappearance.

At all events, the Dominican apostate was handed over to the secular arm only after having been given every chance to escape that rigorous sentence. The Roman Inquisition was much less severe than that of Spain, and Pope Clement VIII was not an inflexible person such as were Paul IV and Sixtus V. But the case of Giordano Bruno, considered in the light of the age, was truly a hopeless one. Contemporaneously, under Queen Elizabeth of England, priests were being decapitated or hanged, drawn and quartered, simply for having celebrated Mass, and yet one never hears the Freethinkers raise the least protest against this strange conception of religious tolerance and respect for opinions manifested by the English Queen. On the other hand, when it is a question of Giordano Bruno, an apostate priest and a propagandist of the most subversive doctrines, an obstinate opponent of all religious truth, invectives violent enough cannot be found to describe "the intolerance of the priests." On June 10, 1889, in the presence of a crowd of some six thousand people bearing red flags, masonic emblems and even the black oriflamme of anarchy, Professor Moleschott, Rector of the University of Rome, delivered a discourse at the unveiling of the Bruno statue, marked, among other felicities, by this now celebrated sentence: "I spit on the putrified corpse of the Catholic Church."

The judges of Giordano Bruno could certainly not have foreseen that their sentence and its aftermath would provoke such consequences at a remote date; but while they did consider, in accordance with the ideas of their time, that an impious impenitent apostate merited to perish by fire, they reached their decision only after having exhausted all the resources of clemency. If other executions took place in Rome, under Clement VIII, of those convicted of obdurate heresy— we are not referring here to the case of Beatrice Cenci, which is irrelevant to our purpose—the reason was that they had been guilty of crimes which, *anywhere else*, would also have been similarly punished.

The case of the other Dominican, Tommaso Campanella, is as interesting as that of Giordano Bruno, though its outcome was less tragic, the Inquisition having in his case shown the utmost indulgence. Tommaso Campanella was born in 1568 at Stilo in Calabria, the terrain of Joachim of Flora and the soil of many philosophic enthusiasms. When, at fifteen, he entered the Dominican Order, he soon became a young prodigy of quick and alert intelligence. He read the *Summa* of Saint Thomas, the works of Albert the Great, the writings of Savonarola, and the more he learned the greater grew his intellectual thirst for greater knowledge. He wrote ceaselessly in verse and in prose.

In Calabria itself, he found a master in the person of the highly erudite Bernardino Telesio, philosopher of his native Cosenza. Telesio was an enemy of Aristotle, and the young Campanella became enamoured of the teachings of the aged philosopher who had retired to his native town to escape the bickering he had encountered because of his anti-aristotelianism. At the age of twenty two, Campanella published his first work: *Philosophia Sensibus Demonstrata,* a defense of Telesio against his eminent adversaries, among whom figured the Jesuits. Although he had finished his studies, taken his Vows and been ordained in the Order of Friars Preachers, he followed the example of Giordano Bruno by leaving the Dominicans and setting off on his travels. For ten years, he traveled in Italy, became acquainted with the men of note in his age—the sculptor Della Porta in Naples, Galileo in Florence, Paolo Sarpi, the Venetian Servite historian highly suspect by the Council of Trent, and even Ferdinand de Medici, Grand Duke of Tuscany.

At that time, for a man of Tommaso's ability, it was not difficult to find a protector and the means to live without excessive material worries. The example of Erasmus and Rabelais, both errant religious, is clear evidence of this. But Campanella was homesick for Calabria, and this proved the occasion for him of an endless series of the greatest misfortunes. The Kingdom of Naples was subjected to the Spanish Crown, and the manner in which it was governed created widespread and lively discontent. Campanella, on his return to Stilo, laid a vast plot to detach Calabria from the Kingdom of Naples. Considerations of a more or less astrological nature were mixed up with the essentially political character of this plot. Like Joachim, his remote compatriot, Campanella was given to the utterance of prophecies. The stars, he said, were proclaiming that the time was ripe for Calabria to become an independent republic. The Turks were to lend assistance.

This plot became widespread, involving Bishops, priests and many religious. An enterprising young man, Maurizio di Rinaldi, a bitter enemy of Spain, was one of the most zealous of Campanella's assistants. Campanella was feeling confident of success, and was reckoning on penetrating the town of Catanzaro, proclaiming his republic there, after the massacre of the notables, including the Bishop, when the plot was discovered by the Spanish authorities. Threatened with arrest, Campanella fled and attempted to embark on a Turkish galley. He was caught, imprisoned, and carried to Naples, where he was tried and had several times to undergo the cruelest of tortures. He was condemned to life imprisonment, and spent nearly twenty

seven years in Neapolitan jails. Until the Viceroy Ossuna fell into disgrace and was recalled from Naples
to Madrid, Campanella's lot was somewhat alleviated,
but Ossuna's successor, Cardinal Zappata, treated him
with increased harshness.

A question of orthodoxy was mixed up with the
accusations of a political kind brought against Campanella and this proved fortunate for him. He had
been imprisoned at Naples in 1600 and was still imprisoned in 1623 when the Roman Inquisition claimed
him to be tried for heresy. This was during the Pontificate of Urban VIII, a genial, enlightened and generous
Pope. Campanella had to answer to the Inquisition for
having written about events to come. When the Calabrian was eventually re-imprisoned on his arrival in
Rome, the Pope set him free, gave him a pension,
authorized him to remain in Rome, and numbered him
among his friends.

Unfortunately, Campanella had powerful enemies
who stirred up the mob against him so that he had to
make his escape in disguise. Again, it was Urban VIII
who saved him, by getting the Count de Noailles, ambassador of Louis XIII, to assist Campanella's escape.
He finally took up residence in Paris, enjoyed the good-
will of the King and of Richelieu to the tune of a
three thousand lire pension, and ended his days there
in peace. The only work of his read today is *Civitas
Solis*, City of the Sun—(there is an English translation
in Morley's "Universal Library") in which he describes
the ideal republic where all is held in common. It has
affinities with Plato's *Republic*, with Saint Thomas
More's *Utopia* and with Fenelon's *Télemaque*. Cam-

panella certainly went through the worst of torments during his Neapolitan captivity, but, by way of balancing the account, and thanks to the magnanimity of Pope Urban, the Roman Inquisition was kind to him.

We come now to another illustrious victim or alleged victim of the Inquisition: the great astronomer, mathematican and genial thinker, Galileo Galilei, compatriot and contemporary of Pope Urban VIII.

Galileo's clash with the Inquisition has had much greater reverberations than that of Campanella or even Giordano Bruno. The great Florentine scholar and astronomer who remained a sincere and fervent Catholic throughout his whole life, has been honored above all others by the enemies of the Church as a noble martyr to science and an innocent victim of clerical fanaticism and ignorance. This legend has won such credence that even Catholic writers are inclined to handle it gingerly, regarding it as a spot on the reputation of the Papacy, over which it is best to draw a discreet veil. Further research has revealed the truth of the matter, however, so that the lies and calumnies for which the name of Galileo has served as pretext, can no longer be repeated.

Within the limits of our present study, we cannot enter into all the ramifications of this complicated affair, in which were involved two eminent Popes (Paul V and Urban VIII), the Grand Duke of Tuscany, the Inquisitors of Florence and of Rome, and the finest of the scholars and theologians of the period.

The sufficient and essential point is that Galileo was not condemned for his anti-Aristotelian theory regarding the rotation of the earth around the sun, but for his obstinacy in mixing sacred and profane science and in setting himself up as a commentator on Holy Scripture. Rome, at that period, was particularly sensitive about lay interference. Repeated efforts had been and were being made to implant Protestantism in Italy, with the result that to abandon to laymen, however learned, the task of interpreting Scripture, was regarded as opening wide the gates to heresy and to its promoters.

The fact is that, nearly a century before Galileo, the Polish priest, Copernicus, who first put forward the heliocentric theory, had dedicated his work on the revolutions of the celestial globes to Pope Paul III, and that his theory had been fully admitted by Clement VII and by Paul III. He had been called to Rome by Leo X, and there he was able to teach openly, among his pupils being Michelangelo and Vittorio Colonna. Furthermore, Copernicus had simply developed a theme which was generally suggested by Cardinal Nicholas de Cusa in his mid-fifteenth century treatise, *De Docta Ignorantia*. However, Copernicus had not denigrators such as Luther, Melanchton, Tycho Brahe, and other eminent represenatives of the Protestant Reformation, to complicate the whole matter. If one will insist on fanaticism, it is not on the Catholic side that it is to be found in this instance. There was a "climate" in Galileo's time different perhaps from that of Copernicus. Protestantism had occasioned such serious dangers for the Church that she was naturally cautious in the extreme about any speculation in matters of religious doctrine, *a fortiori* when such speculation emanated from a layman.

To this we may add a further point. At a time when Scholasticism was in full decadence and showed no promise of its later splendid renaissance under Leo XIII, the Aristotelian professors, who had erected Aristotle into a kind of divinity saw their vested intellectual interests threatened. To them, it was a more serious matter to cast doubts on Aristotle's teachings about anything whatsoever than to deride the Blessed Virgin and the Saints. If we add to all this a certain natural petulance in Galileo's character, a tendency to impose his own way of regarding things, we shall be in a better position to assess the extent of the great Florentine's own responsibility for his troubles with the Holy Office and the Court of Inquisition.

During his two periods in Rome, in 1616 and in 1633, Galileo had dealings with two Popes, Paul V and Urban VIII. The first, the great builder who completed the Basilica of Saint Peter and had his name engraved in the pediment of the facade, was an excellent man, of great generosity, loved by his people. Though he was not an intellectual and took no great interest in cosmic theories, he had boundless admiration for Galileo. When he came to Rome, Paul V gave him a most flattering reception, as did also the members of the Curia, outstanding among them being the illustrious and saintly Cardinal Bellarmine, one of the great saints of the Society of Jesus. However, without becoming unduly involved in the then current controversies about the rotation of the earth, Paul V did not wish to allow laymen to meddle in questions of Scripture. The ravages caused by individual interpretation of the Scriptures were so great and so recent that the Pope felt it an imperative duty to be highly vigilant about such matters.

On March 5, 1616, the year when Galileo came to Rome, the Congregation of the Index, published a decree, in which Galileo was not named directly or by implication, simply condemning Copernicus' *De Revolutionibus Orbium Coelestium* and Diego Zuniga's work on the Book of Job. In other words, it was not forbidden to profess the Copernican doctrine; it was forbidden to teach it publicly because of the connection between the heliocentric theories and certain Scriptural passages, notably the episode of Joshua making the sun to stand still, an episode contradicted by the new doctrine. Galileo had a very cordial interview with Cardinal Bellarmine, in consequence of which a rumor spread that the Florentine had pronounced a formula of abjuration in the Cardinal's presence. The Pope was annoyed by this, and directed Bellarmine to give Galileo a written denial of any such assertion. Throughout the entire affair, Paul V made no pronouncement *ex cathedra*. Properly regarded, it was simply a measure taken to prevent unauthorized persons from intervening in matters concerning the interpretation of the Bible.

There was a lull under Paul's successor, Gregory XV, an able man but a chronic invalid. Yet, despite the fact that Galileo was left in peace, he continued to harass the Court of Rome with requests that the Holy See should give solemn approval to his ideas.

Gregory's reign lasted only two years (1621-1623). His successor was the Florentine Cardinal Maffeo Barberini who, as Urban VIII, was to become one of the greatest Popes. He had long known Galileo and held him in as great esteem as that shown to him by Paul V. More so, indeed, for, besides a natural affinity between them as fellow Florentines, Barberini was intensely interested in theological, philosophical and scientific questions, thereby adding an intellectual affinity.

Although the new Pope's attitude towards Galileo was one of great benevolence, the famous astronomer had declared enemies in Rome, resolutely bent on bringing about his downfall. Generally speaking, these were the peripatetics (Aristotelians) who could not endure the least objection against the teachings of Aristotle. It must be admitted that Galileo acted with an austuteness which came back on himself. Obsessed with effecting the triumph of his heliocentric theories and with reconciling them with Biblical doctrines, he first published a work on the Copernican theory and on the ebb and flow of the sea, and then a *Dialogue* between four speakers comparing the Ptolemaic and Copernican Systems. The latter work contributed greatly to unleashing the storm.

Long efforts had been necessary to obtain the *Imprimatur* from the Master of the Sacred Palace, the Dominican Ricciardi, who was torn between his desire to oblige Galileo and his fear of committing an indiscretion. The book carried a preface calculated to mislead the reader about the author's real intentions. It was printed in Florence, and it provoked violent reactions, though the work was applauded throughout Europe as a literary and scientific masterpiece. A Dominican made a pulpit attack on him, the quarrel grew, and, to put an end to it, Galileo was summoned to Rome to justify himself. In June 1633 he took up residence there with the Florentine Ambassador, and when he was detained for a few days at the palace of the Holy Office, every respect was shown to him.

Judged by the Court of the Inquisition, whose examiners were by no means favorably disposed towards him, he nevertheless received no harsh treatment. He had to pronounce a retractation, and the story is without foundation that after having done so he cried out, in reference to the earth and its rotation, *E pur si muove!*" (And yet it moves!) He then spent some time in Siena with his friend, Archbishop Piccolomini, and spent the rest of his life peacefully at his house in Arcetri, near Florence. The attitude of Urban VIII was one of constant benevolence, despite the fact that he could have taken offense at Galileo's Aristotelian called Simplicio (Simpleton) in the *Dialogue*. Simplicio, a holder of ridiculous opinions, was given certain traits that suggested a caricature of Urban himself, but the Pope was too generous to be peeved at this. His sole concern was with the higher interests of the Church, and he was hostile only towards what could lead the faithful into error in matters of faith.

The Galileo affair has accumulated many legends derogatory of the Church, the Papacy and the Inquisition. A more exact knowledge of the whole matter reduces it to its proper dimensions. Had it not been for Galileo's own imprudent behavior, petulance, and above all his obstinacy in intruding into a branch of studies, that of the interpretation of Scripture, which was outside his scope, he would never have been troubled by the Inquisition.

We have already mentioned Vanini as our final
object of study. In fact, his case does not really come
within the limits of our subject, since he was judged
and sentenced, not by the Roman Inquisition, but by
the *Parlement* of Toulouse. Our only purpose in briefly
recalling the case is to point out the contrast presented
by the procedures of the Inquisition, especially that of
Rome, whose severity was mild by comparison with
that of the civil courts. In connection with the latter,
there are many instances of merciless severity, reaching
at their worst to the most barbarous ferocity.

Giulio Cesare Vanini, born at Naples in 1585, became a secular priest. He also studied medicine, and
was even appointed chief physician to Pope Clement
VIII. An assiduous reader of Pamponazzi and Cardano,
Vanini soon abandoned Christianity. Henceforth, Vanini's only object was to live the gay life of a libertine
untrammelled by any moral scruples.

He led a roving life, and among French libertines
he went under the name Lucilio. As a smoke screen
to his real activities, and as a precaution against trouble
from the authorities, he published books making a
parade of orthodoxy and praising the Jesuits. His
method, however, was ironic. Thus, in his *Ampiteatrum
Divinae Providentiae,* he forcefully presented the ob-
jections of the atheists, and then refuted them with
calculated weakness. The following year, he published
another work characterized by naturalist pantheism
and epicurianism of the grossest kind. Its subject was
the myth of the goddess Nature. Excited by its success,
Vanini lost all restraint and prudence. In 1618, at
Toulouse where he was then residing, he was denounced

as an atheist, arrested, and subjected to a prolonged trial. Having refused to recant, he was condemned to have his tongue cut out and to be burnt at the stake.

Let us make two points clearly. The first, undeniable duty of the Church is to preserve the souls entrusted to her from the contagion of error. Furthermore, error, in the form of heretical ideas or pure negations, is an insidious thing which can infiltrate almost everywhere. It is only by keeping these two points in mind that one can rightly understand the precautions the Church must take if she is to be faithful to her mission. The accomplishments of this mission lies at the root of the entire history of the Roman Inquisition. But since it was a tribunal of fallible men, it was inevitable that not all the judgments pronounced by the Inquisitors throughout the ages were of the purest alloy. Many of them were not.

Nevertheless, and this is the important point for us here, it was the interference of the civil power which largely contributed to vitiate certain proceedings of the Inquisition and the verdicts reached in such cases. We have seen ample evidence of this in the case of the Templars and in that of Joan of Arc.

It remains for us to study another area of the Inquisition, which is at once better known and less understood than the ones we have already dealt with. The rest of the book will be devoted to the Spanish Inquisition, with which the names of Thomas de Torquemada has become so identified as to be its very incarnation.

Part Two

THE SPANISH INQUISITION

CHAPTER ONE

The Origins of the Spanish Inquisition

To understand the essential characteristics of the
Spanish Inquisition and the causes which shaped it,
one must always bear in mind the very special conditions which existed in the Iberian Peninsula before
its unification (except for Portugal) under their Catholic Majesties, Ferdinand of Aragon and Isabella of
Castile, at the time of the *Reconquista*. The brilliant
civilization of the Arab kingdoms, especially in Andalusia, presented a vivid contrast with that of Northern
Spain, as stern and austere as the South was voluptuous.
The caliphs and kings of Cordova and of Granada were
tolerant, their policy being one of "live and let live."

In such an atmosphere of freedom and toleration,
the Jews always occupy a preeminent place in the
center of a disparate society. Active, industrious, hard
working, rich, acutely intelligent, they showed a savoir-
faire far superior to that of the Christians and the

Moors. However, the latter did not lack poets or story-tellers or philosophers. It is sufficient to think of Averroes, the translator of Aristotle into Arabic, to be reminded of the influences which Islam thinkers in Spain must have exercised on Christian thought in the twelfth and thirteenth centuries. At a time in Western Europe when Greek was no longer known, thinkers such as Peter Lombard, Albertus Magnus, and especially Thomas Aquinas, not to mention Siger of Brabant, came to know Aristotle only in a Latin translation of the Arabic translation by Averroes. From many examples among the Jews of Andalusia, one chooses as pre-eminent the philosopher Maimonides, whose work had a vast influence outside Spain and were among the sources used by Saint Thomas Aquinas.

Realizing the mentality of the time, it is easy to understand the suspicion with which the authorized representatives of the Church regarded the influence of these Jews upon the Christians among whom they lived.

Those known as "the old Christians" were Catholics who had continued to live among the Moors after the Arab conquest and had remained faithful to their religious beliefs. One of their characteristics was the practice of a special liturgy, the Mozarabic Liturgy, of which there is now no trace except in a chapel of the Cathedral of Toledo. As the "reconquest" got under way, the question arose of the absorption of non-Christians into the Catholic mass, and this applied much more to the Jews than to the Moors. The baptized Jews were known as *conversos* or *marranos*. Since the Jews occupied an important place in the Spain of this period, acting as bankers, administering the royal finances, practicing medicine, and holding the first rank in the world of business, the sincerity of their practice of Catholicism and of their personal acceptance of the teachings of the Church was a matter of major importance.

There is considerable evidence that among the "conversos" or "marranos" a very great number were Christian in appearance only while continuing to practice in secret the rites of their ancient religion. Some had secret places in their houses where ceremonies inspired by the Talmud were carried out, and where the Crucifix and even consecrated Hosts were profaned. There is never an infallibly guarded secret where many share it, and in due course some alarming denunciations caught the attention of both the civil and the ecclesiastical powers. The matter was referred to Rome, and on November 1st, 1478, Pope Sixtus IV sent a Bull to Spain authorizing their Catholic Majesties to try suspects in accordance with the rules of Canon Law. The Sovereigns were to appoint the Inquisitors, who were to be educated men of high moral standing, offering all the necessary guarantees, and belonging to the secular or regular clergy. The tribunals thus constituted were mixed, being both ecclesiastical and civil. This entirely new type of Inquisition was to have its own laws and be independent of the direct tutelage both of Rome and of the State.

The Sovereigns apponted two Inquisitors, the Dominican Miguel Morillo and Juan de San Martin, and added a fiscal judge and a royal prosecutor. The authorities were ordered to give all necessary support to the members of the new tribunal in carrying out their task, and these members were received with full solemnity at Seville where they installed themselves in the Friary of San Pablo. From then on, things moved briskly. By as early as 1481, twenty four "conversos" of high social position, rich and held in honor, had been imprisoned on the charge of being Judaizers. Such measures provoked widespread reaction. A plot was hatched at Seville, led by Diego Susan, a rich "converso." This plot, aimed at suppressing the Inquisitors and their auxiliaries, was discovered, and early in 1481 four of the leaders were publicly burned alive.

At this early stage of the Spanish Inquisition, Morillo and San Martin showed such zeal and severity that real panic spread among the "marranos" of Seville. Many fled and reached the neighboring frontier of Portugal. Meantime, an outbreak of bubonic plague devastated the capital of Andalusia, leading to a mass exodus of the inhabitants. The Inquisitors themselves took refuge in the little town of Aracena, but continued their brisk activity there: twenty three Judaizers were soon handed over to the secular arm and were burned at the stake.

This persecution was all too much. Informed of what was happening in southern Spain, Sixtus IV intervened vigorously to put an end to such abuses. Converted Jews, declaring themselves good Christians and sincere Catholics, had come to Rome and made their complaint personally to the Pope.

As Ferdinand and Isabella had asked the Pope to set up the Inquisition in the kingdom of Aragon, as an extension of that of Castile, Sixtus IV not only refused but expressed his disapproval of the manner in which the Inquisitors of Seville were fulfilling their mission. As regards the kingdoms of Castile and Leon, the number of Inquisitors were increased and this charge confided to eight Dominicans, among them the General of the Order, Alphonso of San Cebrian and the now famous Thomas de Torquemada whose name was to become synonymous with the Spanish Inquisition.

Without overlooking the importance of the struggle in Spain to secure purity of Christian faith, Sixtus IV constantly insisted that the Canonical precepts should be respected, and that there should be no transgressions of justice. Analogous abuses to those in Seville had occurred in the kingdom of Aragon, where an autonomous Inquisition was functioning, with ramifications in Valencia and in the Balearic islands. Informed by refugees, the Pope intervened just as he had done in Castile, bitterly complaining that the zeal of the judges was motivated less by concern for the salvation of souls than by the desire to possess the property of those condemned.

These sharp exchanges between Rome and the court of their Catholic Majesties led to a common accord. In 1482, a Supreme Council of the Inquisition was instituted which was to form part of the Supreme Council of Castile. An Inquisitor General was to be appointed with authority over Castile, Andalusia, Aragon, Valencia and Catalonia. Through the intervention of Cardinal Gonzales de Mendoza, Thomas de Torquemada was appointed the first Grand Inquisitor of Spain, and thus the Spanish Inquisition was founded and given its definitive form. The abuses against which Sixtus had protested were to diminish gradually.

Some facts of extreme importance must be kept in

mind if we are to have as clear an idea as possible of the origins of the Spanish Inquisition and of the causes which determined its foundation. It cannot be too often stressed that both in Toledo and in Andalusia prior to 1478, the "conversos" had achieved great social importance. Their insolent display of wealth made them unpopular with the Christian population. It was uncertain to what extent a great number of these recently baptized people were sincere in their external profession of the Catholic Faith. Many had preserved hereditary customs concerning diet, the observance of the Sabbath, certain rites before setting out on a journey. But there was more than this. Many nourished a real hatred for everything Christian and, in their secret meetings, they derided the most sacred Christian beliefs, blaspheming by act and word the name of the Redeemer and of His Mother, and, above all else in iniquity, they were credited with performing ritual murders. And rumors fed the fires of bigotry.

Much has been written about this latter point. It has been contested that acts as monstrous as the abduction of a child and its murder, even its crucifixion, could have occurred. Even allowing the largest scope for exaggeration, belief in such heinous crimes was widespread enough to warrant the existence of authentic cases of barbaric treatment inflicted in great secrecy on Christian children abducted and murdered by the Jews. Some incidents on the Jewish side did not help the situation. Take, for example, just one such piece of evidence worthy of credence. In 1468, at Sepulveda, some Jews captured a little boy and, on Good Friday in a remote place, cruelly scourged him and nailed him to a cross in mockery of the Passion of Christ.

The principal author of this horrible crime was the Rabbi of the Synagogue of Sepulveda. His bitterness in inciting his co-religionists to acts of cruelty was increased by irritation at the fact that every year, during Holy Week and especially on Good Friday, Jews were obliged to attend a sermon on the Passion. This obligation also existed in Rome where, on that day, the inhabitants of the ghetto had to assist at a similar ceremony in the little church of Sant' Angelo in Pescheria, situated on the verge of their district.

One can easily imagine the effects produced by the news and rumors, inevitably made more horrific with each telling, of such crimes. In many towns, riots and real progroms occurred, and severe measures were taken following such disturbances. Jews were herded together into special quarters, real ghettos called *Juderias;* the liberal professions, notably medicine and surgery in which they excelled, were prohibited to them. But the threat of fresh troubles continued to weigh on the States of their Catholic Majesties, states then in process of unification.

Such a condition of things, and the resultant social disturbances in certain places and at certain times, undoubtedly, influenced Ferdinand and Isabella and made them wish to establish in their States a jurisdiction with means powerful enough to extirpate the evil threatening domestic peace and religious unity. During the reign of the highly unworthy Henry IV, brother of Isabella, nothing really effective could be done against the danger represented by the Jews and the Judaizers. The same was true during the period after this King's death, when their Catholic Majesties had to war against the Beltrameja, pretender to the throne.

Once masters of the situation, however, they found that there were measures that had to be taken, the one for Aragon and Catalonia, the other for Castile, both together for Andalusia, which had been recently reconquered—or rather, was in process of being so, since the Kingdom of Granada fell only in 1492.

The existing Inquisition, the episcopal Inquisition dependent only on Rome, was somnolent and almost inactive. At Seville, the Dominican Alonso de Hojeda, highly influential with Isabella, showed burning and fanatical zeal in tracking down psuedo-Christians, judaizing Jews, whose secret intrigues he constantly denounced, urging the Queen to take measures he advocated. A chance denunciation came to his assistance. A young Seville aristocrat was courting a girl whose father was a "converso." In this girl's house, he listened unseen to things said there which disturbed him very much. He revealed all this to Alonso, who hastened to make use of it, and, to a considerable extent, it was through pressure from this rigorous Dominican that Isabella decided to ask Sixtus IV to authorize the institution of an inquisitorial tribunal of a new kind, created for purposes both religious *and* political.

It is a fact that there were certain abuses and acts of excessive severity incompatible with justice and charity, committed particularly in Seville and in other parts of Andalusia, but elsewhere too, in Toledo and in Aragon, during the early years of the Spanish Inquisition.

Morillo and San Martin began by summoning a great number of suspects to appear before them. These were invited to admit their faults, through which admission they could be reconciled to the Church by means of a penance more or less severe according to the gravity of their case. "Old Christians" were invited to denounce suspects about whom they had precise information, under pain of excommunication if they failed to do so. The vast majority of those who presented themselves before the Inquisitors received a relatively light sentence, ranging from public flagellations which the penitents were to impose on themselves during a procession to such things as the wearing of a badge, the recitation for a certain time of the penitential psalms or other prayers, the fulfillment of a more or less arduous or expensive pilgrimage. Those convicted of more serious faults could incur temporary or life imprisonment.

There remained those whose obstinate refusal to repent even under torture, gave the ecclesiastical judges no option but to hand them over to the secular arm. Such were then sentenced to the stake. This punishment in conformity with the manners of the time was not, as we know, peculiar to Spain. On the other hand, the special Iberian character of the whole affair was the long ceremony, the details of which we shall give later, preceding and accompanying the execution of the condemned. These macabre disgraceful spectacles were called *autos da fe* (acts of faith).

In order to better understand the Spanish Inquisition, it should be emphasized that its establishment in Spain was not aimed at the Jews who remained faithful to their own religion. The object of the Inquisition was to prosecute those Jews (*conversos* or *marranos*) who simulated a conversion to the Christian faith for the sole purpose of gaining social and financial advantages.

Having said something about the Dominicans Alonso de Hojeda, Morillo and San Martin, we shall now take a closer look at the Grand Inquisitor himself, Thomas de Torquemada.

CHAPTER TWO

Thomas de Torquemada, Grand Inquisitor of Spain

From what we have already said, it is clear that the Spanish Inquisition did not come into existence (about 1480) without creating difficulties, notably between Sixtus IV and their Catholic Majesties. Behind all the actions of the Pope was the desire that a certain *status quo* should be maintained, the new Inquisitors being placed under the tutelage and authority of the Bishops in accordance with the pattern of inquisitorial organization as then existing. On the other hand, Ferdinand and Isabella, more direct and more immediately interested witnesses of what was occurring in their States, urged something else. It was their wish that a new kind of Inquisition should be set up to deal with the Judaizing "conversos," to lead them back into the right way, or to suppress them if they obstinately continued in their errors and in their secret and blasphemous practices.

The special quality of this new Inquisition was to be its *complete autonomy;* it was to be totally independent of the episcopal power—regarded more or less as somnolent—and it was to give the Crown direct assistance in the work of unifying and re-Christianizing the country. The Spanish rulers succeeded in getting what they wanted. Certain initial excesses of severity were corrected, and the appointment of eight Inquisitors of Castile, while strengthening the institution, enabled one of the eight to acquire an ascendancy and an authority calculated to make him the very incarnation of the Spanish Inquisition. This man was the Dominican, Thomas de Torquemada.

The enemies of the Spanish Inquisition and the writers of fiction, by their lying allegations and more or less wild fantasies have created a picture of Torquemada as one of the most insensate torturers in history. The result is a ludicrously inaccurate caricature of this energetic Religious.

Thomas de Torquemada (1420-1498) was the son of Don Pedro Ferdinando, lord of Torquemada (Valladolid), and nephew of Cardinal Juan de Torquemada, an eminent theologian and Dominican, champion of Saint Thomas Aquinas, upholder of the doctrine of the Immaculate Conception later defined (December 8, 1854) by Pope Pius IX. Juan de Torquemada (1388-1468) also vigorously sustained the principle of Papal Infallibility against those who sought to place the authority of the ecumenical council above that of the Pope.

At an early age, Thomas followed his uncle's example and became a Dominican of the Priory of Saint Paul in his native Valladolid. His rare mental ability led to his being elected Prior of Santa Cruz in Segovia, to which post he was re-elected several times because of his holiness and of the tact with which he carried out his duties. In addition, he was a severely austere man, carrying to extremes the spirit of mortification and of poverty. Because of these exceptional qualities, Torquemada was honored by being appointed spiritual director of the Infanta Isabella of Castile. At that time, the Princess still lived at the court of her brother, Henry IV, of deplorable memory. When she eventually ascended the throne of Castile, Torquemada continued as her director and was thus enabled to add the weight of his influence to Hojeda's petiitons that the Queen should take measures to extirpate the evil created by psuedo-converts from Judaism.

It was in 1483 that Pope Sixtus decided to give definitive form to the new Inquisition organized in Spain. In her approaches to the Holy Father, Isabella had stressed the need to place at the head of the new institution an Inquisitor General with supreme authority over the different Tribunals of the entire peninsula. The virtues of Torquemada fitted him for the heavy responsibilities of such a post, and accordingly he was proposed by Ferdinand and Isabella. The Pope appointed him Grand Inquisitor of Castile, by the Bull dated October 17, 1483, but soon his powers were extended to Aragon, and, in practice, to the whole country.

With the appointment of Torquemada, the Spanish Inquisition entered upon a new phase. His extraordinary talents and power eventually raised him to such eminence that he became a kind of rival to the Sovereigns themselves.

An organizer of great ability, the Grand Inquisitor began by setting up four fixed tribunals—at Seville, Cordova, Jaen, and Villa Real (Ciudad Real). There were already Inquisitors in Toledo, Valladolid, Avila, Segovia, previously appointed by the Pope and not always inclined to show entire submission to Torquemada's orders. Those who seemed more or less restive were quickly deposed and replaced by more manageable people.

Since the Spanish Inquisition, in its new form, had become an institution as much political as religious, the man who directed and animated it had necessarily to remain in constant contact with the Rulers. Torquemada continued, therefore, to reside at the Court after having taken up his new position. Previously, their Catholic Majesties were assisted by four Royal councils, with whom they discussed affairs of state. A fifth was now added to deal with questions concerning the Inquisition. This was composed of three royal counsellors and two of Torquemada's assessors. The President of this council—the Suprema—was the Grand Inquisitor himself.

In October 1484, shortly after the creation of the Fifth Council, Torquemada called to Toledo his own appointed Inquisitors of Seville, Cordova, Jaen and Villa Real, in order to give them his instructions and to clarify everything concerning the activity and methods of the Spanish Holy Office. These instructions, comprising twenty eight articles, were published in Madrid about a century later.

We have had occasion to refer to the *Practica Inquisitionis* of the Dominican Bernard Gui, which goes back to 1320. About the middle of the fourteenth century and under the inspiration of this book, Nicholas Eymerich wrote a long *Directorium Inquisitorium*. Eymerich was a native of Aragon. Those whom he sought to prosecute were heretics properly so called, as had been and was being done in southern France, Lombardy and elsewhere.

Torquemada no doubt used Eymerich's Directorium when he drew up his own *Instructions*, adapting the measures taken to the particular circumstances of time and place which had occasioned the new Spanish Inquisition. These *Instructions* reflect the meticulous and methodical mind of Torquemada. Anxiety to lead the guilty to recognize their errors and to become reconciled with the Church, is evident throughout all the twenty eight articles. We shall attempt to summarize them here.

The Inquisitors appointed to a diocese, a town, a village, after having checked with the ecclesiastical and civil authorities, are to assemble the population, clergy and laity, in the principal church, where they hear a sermon from some notable preacher. Then all are to take an oath upon the Cross to assist the Inquisition in its task. The text of the censures incurred by those who contest the validity of the powers of the Holy Office, is then read aloud.

There follows an interval of thirty or forty days to enable those guilty of heresy or apostasy or observance of Jewish or other rites contrary to the Christian religion, to confess their sins, with the full assurance of being received with charity if they show themselves to be sincere by keeping back nothing relevant about themselves or any other guilty party. Apart from exceptionally serious cases, these people will not suffer imprisonment or fines or confiscation of goods. Letters patent, bearing the Royal seal, will attest the reality of their reconciliations. Penitents are to present their confession in writing before witnesses; they will be minutely questioned to establish all the circumstances of their lapses. After that, the Inquisitors demand a public abjuration, but they are instructed to use the utmost possible leniency. If the sinner has never allowed his sin to become known to others, he is to be dispensed from public penitence and absolved in secret.

Here, Torquemada's severity increases. Even when reconciled, repentant heretics are not to exercise any public function, and many of the professions are closed to them. Neither may they wear costly clothes, ornaments or anything made of gold, bear arms or ride a horse. Those who present themselves to the Inquisitors after the period of grace may be reconciled but are to receive sentences fixed by the judges. Since their property will have been confiscated, these sentences cannot be of a monetary kind. Imprisonment, even life imprisonment, is to be imposed in accordance with the nature of the case.

The children of heretics (i.e. those below the age of twenty), who come forward to declare the errors into which their parents led them, are to be treated with particular leniency. The mere fact of having fallen into heresy and of having apostatized, implies for the guilty the loss of their goods and of the right to administer them. These confiscated goods go to the Royal treasury. When a heretic is arrested after having been denounced, but shows a desire to be reconciled, he may be absolved but he incurs a sentence of life imprisonment—a sentence which may be commuted to a lighter one, according to the case.

In cases where the Inquisitors are conscientiously sure that the penitent is merely simulating contrition, he may be handed over to the secular arm. Even a reconciled heretic may be re-tried if it is later established that his repentance was mere pretence. In the case where an accused obstinately denied his guilt even up to the pronouncing of sentence, and continues to proclaim himself a good Catholic, the Church will show no mercy towards him if his crime is juridically proved beyond the shadow of doubt. In such a case, of course, the Church must act with extreme prudence in order to avoid condemning someone who is the innocent victim of interested witnesses. Furthermore, it may be that the crime is only half proved, in which case the accused may be put to the torture. If he then makes an admission, he must ratify that confession in writing. If he refuses to do so, a public abjuration may be demanded of him or he may be again tortured.

Here arises a factor which cannot fail to awaken some perplexity. In view of the fact that certain witnesses have been killed or wounded by heretics for having made depositions in an inquisitorial trial, the accused may not be shown the written acts containing the details of the imputations made against him. He will know these imputations only by what he is told about them, without being able to find out who are his accusers. On the other hand, he may have legal help, paid for by himself or by the Royal treasury if his goods have been confiscated. As a general rule, the Inquisitors themselves are to do the questioning. If an accused person is put to the torture, an Inquisitor must be present. If the accused is away when he is cited, a notice on the Church door will summon him to present himself within thirty days, in default of which he will be judged contumacious.

If a writ reveals that a dead person has lived as an undetected heretic, his body is to be exhumed and burnt. The deceased person may be defended by his children. At the request of their rulers, the Inquisitors may operate within the domains of nobles, in exactly the same way as they do within territories directly dependent on the Crown. When heretics handed over to the secular arm have been put to death, it is for the Inquisitors to see to the children and to ensure that they will be brought up in accordance with the principles of Catholicism. The royal charity may come to their help. Provision is made for restitution of goods, in certain cases, to a reconciled sinner whose property had been confiscated for the crime of heresy. The slaves of condemned heretics are to be set free, and they can never be given back.

The Inquisitors and their assistants are forbidden, under pain of excommunication, to accept gifts from those with whom they have any official dealings. Besides the Canonical sanction, those guilty of such conduct must make restitution to twice the value of the gift or gifts. Torquemada makes an urgent appeal for the greatest possible harmony among the members of the tribunal and among the lower personnel. If a question arises which is not provided for by the regulations, the Inquisitors are to seek inspiration from existing laws, having in view only the service of Christ and of the Sovereigns.

The above is a careful summary of the twenty-eight

articles of the regulations drawn up, with help from the works of Bernard Gui and in particular of Eymerich, by "the Prior of Santa Cruz," Grand Inquisitor of Spain. He was to complete them later, in 1488 and 1498, but only by the addition of minor details. From our summary it can be readily seen that Torquemada left nothing to chance or to whim. The whole of Spain was covered by a finely meshed net, and it was very difficult for a guilty person to escape such vigilant justice. The severity of the great Dominican did not, however, preclude a concern for charity and equity. Generally speaking, it was with the Judaizing "conversos" that the tribunal of the Holy Office was preoccupied. To make a fair judgment of the work of Torquemada, one must constantly remember the particular conditions prevailing in fifteenth century Spain, when Ferdinand of Aragon and Isabella the Catholic were completing the work of unification and were about to put the seal on that work by the capture of Granada in 1492.

Spain as we know, had been for many centuries a choice ground for Jews and Moors. It is worthy of note, that the royal severity and that of Torquemada was exercised only against pseudo-Christians, not against those non-Christians who were faithful to their ancestral religion and who were living side by side with Catholics without trying to use any influence on them. The Judaizing "conversos" were in a totally different position. The very fact of their belonging to the Church by Baptism brought them into much more direct contact with the Christian element of the population. There were many marriages between baptized Jews and "old Christians." If the former—and the case was much more frequent than might be supposed—

remained secretly attached to their ancestral beliefs, one can appreciate the influence they must have exercised, especially over their children.

Above all, when one is considering the Spanish Inquisition as a whole, it must be remembered that this was a royal tribunal, created to meet a political danger in a country and at a period when religious unity was the fundamental basis of the social order. The choice of Torquemada proves of itself alone the concern of Ferdinand and Isabella to secure the collaboration of an upright and incorruptible man, free of all temporal interest, exempt from any political ambition, and having nothing in view except the good of the Church and of his country. The very barbarities of the Spanish Inquisition are the reflection of the manners of the age, and when the Inquisitors ordered the torturing of an accused person, they did so simply in order to conform to the prescriptions of the civil law.

In his *Lettres à Un Gentilhomme Russe sur l'Inquisition Espagnole*, Joseph de Maistre puts these points clearly and well. One point, in particular, stands out. "I believe," he writes, "that the heresiarch, the obstinate heretic and the propagator of heresy, should undoubtedly be numbered among the greatest criminals. If we are deceived about this, it is because we cannot help judging in accordance with the indifference of our own age in matters of religion; whereas we ought to take as our measure the ancient zeal, which some are pleased to call *fanaticism*, though it has nothing to do with that quality. The modern armchair sophist is scarcely perturbed that the arguments of Luther produced the Thirty Years' War; but the legislators of past ages, aware of what these pernicious doctrines could involve, very rightly punished with death a crime capable of overthrowing the very foundation of Society and bathing mankind in blood."

Joseph de Maistre takes a point of view which proves very difficult for the majority of people today. The accepted principle is that every man is free to profess what opinions he chooses, and to spread those opinions. Any measure taken to prevent the propagation of error, is immediately condemned as intolerance. But that was an intolerable age. This is to ignore one of the fundamental points, not only of Catholicism but quite simply of the Gospel itself, in which we find Our Lord enjoining the cutting off of a hand or the plucking out of an eye which is a cause of scandal. Above all, it is especially relevant not to lose sight of one supremely important point. No one would deny the errors committed through excess of zeal—through fanaticism, if you will—by certain Inquisitors who were more concerned with carrying out the wishes of the civil power than uniquely preoccupied with the religious point of view and the interests of the Church.

And yet, it remains a fact that Spain never knew anything like the atrocious and fratricidal slaughter of the Wars of Religion in France during the sixteenth century, or the upheavals for more than a century in religion-torn sixteenth century Germany. While confusion reigned beyond the Pyrenees, the Spain of Charles V, of Philip II and their successors, was extending its reign beyond the ocean into the countries of the New World, in which she was planting the Cross, and putting, in place of the barbaric and bloody cults of the Aztecs and the Incas, the religion of the love of Christ. And this internal peace which the metropolis enjoyed through the maintenance of her religious unity, made possible the full blossoming of the *Siglo de Oro,* thanks to which Spain was able to furnish one of the richest parts of the artistic and spiritual patrimony of the western and Christian world. We shall consider, in a later chapter, the extent of the danger from which the Inquisition defended Spain, in the time of the Catholic Kings.

The Tragedy of Saragossa:
Saint John de Arbues

The efforts demanded at Seville to enable the Inquisition, then in its beginnings, to continue its task, clearly shows that the Judaizers did not intend to submit to prosecution without hitting back.

Very soon after Torquemada had taken office, Spain was divided into different zones in relation to the activity of the Holy Office. In 1482, the Inquisition was established at Cordova, then at Toledo, Calahorra, and later on in other dioceses of the North.

In 1484, during an assembly of the Cortez at Saragossa, it was decided that the Inquisition should be extended to the Kingdom of Aragon. Two eminent men— Peter de Arubes, Canon of the metropolitan Cathedral, and the Dominican Gaspar Juglar—were appointed to preside there. Their collaborators took the oath, and the Inquisition was very soon in active existence.

As regards religion, the Kingdom of Aragon was

somewhat uneasy. The "conversos" there were numerous, rich, educated and powerful. Many of them were still secretly attached to the faith of their ancestors, and what had happened in Andalusia had put them on their guard. They were determined to use every means to shackle the new tribunal. Vigorous protests were made about the unjust confiscation of the property of those suspected of heresy, and about the fact that the accused had no means of knowing the names of their denouncers. These regulations, it was alleged, were unjust. The "new Christians" began by sending two ambassadors to the King, an Augustinian and a jurist called Peter de Luna—the latter having the same name as the celebrated Avignon anti-Pope called Benedict XIII (1394-1424) who was also a native of Aragon.

This was unsuccessful and, with the imminence of danger, the party decided to use violence. Some of the richest and most influential of the "conversos" came together secretly in Saragossa, and decided that the only effective remedy was to assassinate the Grand Inquisitor Peter de Arbues, thereby creating terror and securing the abolition of the tribunal. This was clearly an insane scheme which, if carried out, could only flout the King and provoke merciless reprisals.

The conspirators assembled at the house of Luis de Santangel in the parish of Saint Felix in Saragossa. The list of those who attended showed that they were men of high social standing. One of them addressed the assembly as follows: "We must be little men indeed if we cannot cope with the task of getting rid of two or three Inquisitors, thereby preventing the creating of this tribunal." He went on to offer one hundred, or even two hundred gold florins to anyone who would do the deed.

Reunions multiplied, and in great secrecy, the date for carrying out the plot was fixed for September 15, 1485, between eleven o'clock and midnight, the time at which the members of the Chapter were accustomed to go to the Cathedral to chant Matins. Leaving at the church door a small group of masked and armed men, three of the conspirators with two servants stole into the cathedral under cover of darkness, and lay in wait for the moment when Peter de Arbues would enter to take his place in the choir.

The Inquisitor soon arrived, and went to kneel before the chapel of the Blessed Sacrament. While the Canon in choir dress was reciting the *Ave Maria*, Abadia, one of the conspirators, said to his companion Vidan, "Strike him, the traitor!" Vidan dealt him a blow on the head wtih his sword. John de Arbues attempted to reach the choir, but another conspirator, John de Esperandeo, struck him with the sword, and the unfortunate Inquisitor fell down on the spot that was to be his burial place. The assassins fled when they saw the Canon lying on the ground. The other clergy rushed in when they heard the commotion. They carried the wounded man to his house, and two surgeons, urgently summoned, could do nothing for him. John de Arbues died two days later, without having uttered a single complaint.

As soon as he heard of this crime, the Archbishop of Saragossa, Alonso of Aragon, went around the town on horseback urgently restraining the people for fear a general massacre of the Judaizers would ensue. In return, he promised that justice would be done without delay. The Spanish Inquisition delegated its powers to a Cistercian, John de Colmenares, Abbot of Aguilar, to a Dominican, John de Colivera, and to a Canon of the metropolis, John de Alarcon. These three men took up residence in the Aljaferia, the ancient palace of the Moorish Kings, and henceforward this became the seat of the Holy Office for the capital of the Kingdom of Aragon. The investigation began immediately. It was established that the Inquisitor's death had been promoted by four conspirators, Luis Santangel, Francisco de Santa Fe, Alonso Sanchez and Peter de Almazan. The murderers were identified as John de Esperandeo, Mateo Raem, John de la Abadia, Vidal Duran and the latter's equerry, Tristancio.

Esperandeo was declared "an enfeoffed and circumcised Jew." His hands were cut off before the Cathedral porch, and then he was led to the marketplace where a scaffold had been prepared. His head was cut off, and his body was dismembered and thrown into the common sewer. His two hands were nailed to the door of the palace of the Deputation. Vidal Duran had a similar fate. Gaspar de Santa Cruz, who had offered a large sum for the assassination, succeeded in escaping to France. Both he and Martin de Santangel were burned in effigy. Another Judaizer, Peter of Exea, was burned alive, for having promoted the murder. Another, Francisco de Santa Fe, having been incarcerated in the prisons of the Inquisition, flung himself to his death from the top of a high tower. His corpse was recovered and the bones were thrown into the waters of the Ebro river.

The murdered Canon was avenged with even greater cruelty. The merciless character of this repression, of its kind unique in the annals of the Spanish Inquisition, is explained from the viewpoint of the civil power—the guilty having been handed over to the secular arm—by the nature itself of the crime. The Tribunal of the Holy Office confined itself to declaring the accused guilty of heresy, as proved by the murder of the Inquisitor. As for the methods of punishment, it was the civil power alone which decided these, in accordance with the laws then in force. But no doubt, the Inquisition approved of the civil punishments and must bear the blame.

Peter Arbues de Epila quickly began to be the object of a cult. Miracles were claimed through his intercession and the Inquisitor came to be regarded as a martyr. He was buried at the spot where he had been murdered, and in 1487 Isabella had a magnificent tomb erected there. Some two centuries later he was beatified by Alexander VII. In the nineteenth century, he was canonized by Pius IX.

CHAPTER FOUR

Methods and Activity of the Spanish Inquisition

Up to this point, we have been dealing more particularly with Jews converted to Catholicism for reasons of interest, the "conversos" who remained interiorly attached to the old dispensation, pseudo-Christians known as "Judaizers" with whom the Inquisition was especially concerned. Besides these, there were "conversos" from Mohammedanism, known as "moriscos," who were particularly numerous in the old Kingdom of Granada, the last rampart of Islam.

These "conversos" were following all kinds of professions, in which they usually showed great skill. They devoted themselves to agriculture and to the multiple branches of craft and industry, silk making being one of them. Before the entry of Ferdinand and Isabella into Granada, on January 6, 1492, a treaty known as "the Granada capitulations" was signed at the gates of the city, by which the Sovereigns agreed to allow full liberty of conscience to the Moors. They were to be free to sell their property and to load their movables on to large ships placed at their disposal to carry them to the Barbary coast. Those who opted to remain would not be obliged to wear any distinguishing badge, nor would any financial charges be imposed on them for the upkeep of Christian churches, their obligation being confined to payments in support of their own Mosques. This did not imply that their Catholic Majesties were not concerned to establish religious unity, little by little, in their States; but their representatives, ecclesiastical and lay, received instructions inviting them to use great moderation. The choice of the new Archbishop of Granada, Hernando de Talavera, was an excellent one. He was a man of deep piety and of exemplary life, his master aim being to lead the Moors to the Christian Faith by mildness and persuasiveness. He was very successful in this, and was highly venerated and loved by the Moors.

The charge of captain general was given to Don Inigo Lopez de Mendoza, with the title of Viceroy. An adroit politician, he established himself as a protector of the Moors.

The early stages of the aggregation of the old Kingdom of Granada to the Estates of the Spanish Royalty were, therefore, exempt from violent upheavals. In 1494, however, things took a turn for the bad. Wishing to lighten the heavy burden of Archbishop Hernando de Talavera, Ferdinand and Isabella sent him as coadjutor the celebrated Archbishop of Toledo, Francisco Jiminez de Cisneros, whose standing at the Court was very high. Unfortunately, he was a haughty man not given to accommodating to the views of others.

He chose to impose Baptism by force on the Moors rather than follow the Talavera line. These measures naturally turned the Moors against him. He ordered the seizure from the Moors of a number of precious, richly bound books dealing with doctrinal questions, and had them publicly burned. These measures provoked disturbances, and only the intervention of Talavera saved Cisneros from being molested.

Nothing daunted, Cardinal Cisneros sought and obtained from the King and Queen a formal order that the Moors should accept Baptism or emigrate to the Barbary States. These forced Baptisms of the Moors, had only a very qualified value, with the result that the new converts from Islam remained for the most part as attached to their original faith as the "conversos" from Judaism remained to theirs.

It became evident that the coexistence of Catholics and pseudo-convert "moriscos" grew daily more and more difficult. This situation led to the expulsion of the Jews and the Moors from the Kingdom. This persecution will ever be listed among the cruelties of the Inquisition. It was not until 1608, in the reign of Philip III, that the first minister of the King secured a royal decree definitively banishing the moriscos from Spain and causing them to set sail for the Barbary States. A formal order was given not to molest them in any way. Since these moriscos had developed highly successful agricultural methods, six families in every hundred dispossessed in each district of the old Kingdom of Valencia were retained to initiate the new inhabitants into the art of cultivating the many crops that ensured the wealth of that fertile province.

It is undeniable that the elimination of the Moors

and the Jews from Spain, by successive waves, impoverished the country. But the Inquisitors who presided over this immense "purgation" had a purpose other than that of safeguarding economic interests. They sought to preserve the purity of the Catholic faith.

The Spanish Inquisition was governed by the Grand Inquisitor, whose powers were practically absolute, assisted by his council. No sentence could be carried out before ratification by the Council. It often happened that the Grand Inquisitor modified a given sentence referred to him, often in the direction of leniency and even of pardon.

Every year, the regional Inquisitors were obliged to make a complete tour of their alloted territory. In the course of this tour, they carried out extremely close enquiries, and showed perfect knowledge of the beliefs, usages, customs and traditions of those who seemed to them worthy of prosecution, whether such people were Judaizers, or externally conforming Moors, or later, in the second quarter of the sixteenth century, more or less cryptic adherents of the doctrines of Luther, or finally, members of the more specifically Spanish sect of "Enlightened" or Alumbrados. When reading the general Edicts of the Holy Office, one is struck not only by the Inquisitors' breadth of information, but also by the very special importance they attached to everything immediately or remotely concerning the Jews. In fact, the Spanish Inquisition had been founded especially to combat and to prevent the Judaization of the country. The Holy Office also kept a very diligent eye on the practices of sorcery, at a time when such

practices enjoyed a widespread popularity, and prosecuted those who indulged in them.

When the Inquisitors had proclaimed their arrival
in a certain place, anyone who could assist them in
their inquiries by supplying information of any relevant kind was bound to do so under pain of excommunication. It was the duty of all who knew themselves to be guilty, to come forward freely and make
a sincere confession of their faults. They would thus
avoid prison, confiscation of property, and of course,
torture and committal to the secular arm and to death
by fire. In the case of a free and unconstrained confession of relapse into faults previously freely admitted,
the judges of the Holy Office were content with in-
flicting a public penance for some specified time.

All the guilty had not the courage or the will to
reveal themselves in this way. Only rarely, however,
did any such transgressions escape completely the in-
vestigations of the Inquisitors. Once denounced, the
suspects were arrested, imprisoned and interrogated.
They were given every opportunity, however, to prove
their innocence or to retract and to give full guarantees
of true repentance.

There were nevertheless cases in which the accused
persisted in denying the charge, despite the fact that
the Inquisitors had ample evidence of their guilt. Then
recourse could be had to torture. We have already said
enough about these practices, which were in conformity
with the usages and manners of the period. What we
would stress here is that, in the case of *all* the courts
of the Holy Office, including that of the Spanish Inquisition, the accused was led into the torture chamber
only after having been many times exhorted to tell

the truth. Before being definitely handed over to the torturers, he was again exhorted, and shown the instruments of torture so that he might realize to what he was exposing himself by obstinately denying a charge which the Inquisitors had good reasons, or at least strong presumptions, for regarding as true. Such was medieval justice!

As soon as the accused under torture declared his willingness to confess, the torture ended and he was taken to a neighboring room where, in the presence of the judge, a clerk of the court wrote down his statements. In Spain, as everywhere else, it was laid down that the torture was to entail neither the death nor the mutilation of the accused. One cannot deny the barbarity of such procedures, which, unfortunately, with a refinement of cruelty, have reappeared in our own scientific age. It is none the less true, however, that sectarian hatred of the Church has led some to indulge wildly in fiction about the tortures inflicted by the Spanish Inquisition, and that genuine and severely exhaustive historical research presents an entirely different picture.

Similarly, the Spanish prisons of the Holy Office have often been described as filthy, dark, airless holes, in which the prisoners crouched like some kind of base animals. Some indeed, were appalling. Sometimes the prisoners were kept in cells in the same palace used by the Inquisitors. Strict instructions were formally issued to the custodians: they were to see that nothing was lacking to their prisoners in the way of food, clothes, and whatever other necessaries they wanted in their cells. The prisoners were rarely in solitary confinement. They could have books for their entertainment or to help them to prepare their defense. They could have an advocate of their own choosing. These privileges were paid for by the prisoners themselves.

While the accused awaited trial after having been arrested when there were serious presumptions of their guilt (and then only), the judges would study the cases submitted. Their means of information were, above all, the evidence given and the charges laid by other people. This gives rise to the delicate question of the secrecy preserved vis-a-vis the accused about these charges. The procedure has been greatly discussed, as we have already said. The accused persons would often protest against imputations whose source was concealed from them, thereby preventing them from confronting their alleged calumniators face to face. On the other hand, to give such information to the accused might well lead to vengeance by the accused or by his family. The secrecy was dictated by a great number of these cases of *vendetta*, in which the authors of these reports to the Inquisitors had been assassinated, even in a church. Clearly, each system had its disadvantages, and, if we are to judge the matter fairly, account must be taken of the violence of unleashed passions.

When the cases were concluded, the accused persons having been questioned and the advocates having delivered their speeches, the sentence of condemnation or acquittal had to be announced solemnly and publicly in the course of an *auto da fe*. At the outset, let us say that these solemn ceremonies at which crowds were present, had not the cruel character so often attributed to them. There was neither scaffold nor executioner present. Those (and they were rare) who had been sentenced to be handed over to the civil power were taken, after the ceremonies, to a place remote from that of the *auto da fe*. This place, called the *quemadero*, was reserved for executions by fire.

The *auto da fe*, properly so called, consisted of a very spectacular display, announced with trumpets the day before, in which the civic authorities took part and which was watched by all the inhabitants. It began with a solemn procession of the representatives of the different Religious Orders and the members of the Confraternities, the eminences of the Court of Inquisition with the "familiars" of the Holy Office, and the accused, some wearing a kind of scapular called a *sanbenito*, others wearing an iron collar or some other symbolic object around their necks. The civil authorities walked in line after the secular clergy.

The procession advanced slowly, with lighted candles, to the main place where a huge carpeted platform had been set up, on which were placed armchairs for the Inquisitors and a long table for the recording clerks of the court. When all the assembly had taken the assigned places, a priest celebrated Mass on an altar placed on the edge of the platform. This was followed by an appropriate sermon, which led up to the pronouncing of the sentence passed by the Court of the Inquisition against the heretics or presumed heretics who were present. Some were absolved who had been proved innocent or judged worthy of pardon. Others, more guilty, received various punishments—a public penance, a fine, the making of a sometimes painful and expensive pilgrimage, temporary or life imprisonment. Finally, the small group of the relapsed were handed over to the secular arm to be taken away to the place of execution.

The ceremony took place under the emblem of the standard and cross of the Inquisition, the color being green, symbolizing hope!

As we have seen, very special conditions distinguished the Spanish Inquisition, closely linked as it was with the crown, although this did not affect the independence of the Grand Inquisitor when there was question of taking serious decisions. However, it would be a mistake to suppose that the Court of the Holy Office, instituted in Spain, was in any way withdrawn from the authority and control of the Holy See. Rome has always taken an interest in any steps taken anywhere to maintain the purity of the faith. Many appeals were made from the Spanish Inquisition to Rome, by accused persons, and when this occurred, all proceedings were suspended. Cases could be quoted in which sentences passed in Spain were squashed on appeal to Rome.

On the other hand, however, when the authority of the King of Spain extended in time to Sicily, Sardinia, Naples and Lombardy, the guilty or those presumed so, who came into the hands of the Roman Holy Office, were tried by the Spanish Inquisitors. This was attended with some unpleasantness. There were instances where the Spanish Inquisitors showed an excessively authoritarian attitude, a haughtiness and even insolence which greatly offended the Archbishops or Bishops of the dioceses concerned, and this in a period of history when punctilious behavior, even to excess, was the order of the day. In this connection, one could cite a very curious letter from an Archbishop of Oristano in Sardinia to the Spanish Grand Inquisitor, bitterly complaining about the lack of courtesy shown to him in his own small archiepiscopal town by the representatives of the Spanish Inquisition.

Apart from the *auto da fe* described above, the Holy Office carried out, several times a year, what was known as "the publication of the decree of faith". This publication, performed with great ceremony and featuring an appropriate sermon, took place in several churches of the same town—at Madrid, for instance, on certain days announced in advance to the people. The decree of faith was accompanied by anathemas pronounced against those who professed heterodox opinions. On such days, the members of the Court, finely arrayed, went in procession to the church where the ceremony was to take place. On occasion, the decree of faith was read in one church and the anathema pronounced a little later, in another.

The Court of the Spanish Inquisition received many tokens of the highest reverence from the public powers and from the Sovereign himself. Any magistrate, unconnected with the Holy Office, was strictly forbidden to deal with anything concerning heresy and crimes affecting the purity of the Catholic Faith. If, as we have seen did occur, a member of the inquisitorial court committed reprehensible acts or abused his authority, the King would always address himself with the utmost respect and reverence to the Grand Inquisitor in order that he might take the necessary steps to restore proper order. In other words, it was made possible for the Inquisitors and their assistants to accomplish their delicate mission unhampered since they also enjoyed unique privileges, some of which had been directly conceded to them by the Holy See, as witness the Brief *De protegendis* of Pope Saint Pius V.

From this period until the end of the eighteenth century, we find the Spanish Inquisition as one of the dominant institutions in the Kingdom.

CHAPTER FIVE

The Inquisition and the Reformation:
The Alumbrados: Some Famous Cases

Up to this point, we have been dealing with the war waged by the Court of the Holy Office in Spain against the "conversos" and the "moriscos". The Inquisition, however, took on further tasks.

In the sixteenth century, when Europe was torn apart by the Lutheran Reform and the religious unity of the West was destroyed, the Inquisition saved Spain from the contagion. Without its vigilance and severity, the Kingdom of Philip II and his successors—the danger had already existed under Charles V—would have known the horrors of a war more or less similar to that of sixteenth century France. The doctrines of Luther, and later on those of Calvin, did not find as propitious a soil in Castile, in Andalusia, in Galicia, in Aragon, or in Catalonia, as they did in certain regions of Poitou or of Southern France. Nevertheless, they did find adherents in those provinces, especially among the nobility and even in a certain number of religious communities.

From 1523, the Inquisitors took measures against the circulation of Luther's works in Spain. But the danger continued. In Holland, a mass of propaganda was prepared, with texts translated into Castilian to be surreptitiously introduced into the Iberian peninsula. In London, too, Bibles were printed in the vernacular, and carefully concealed in bales of merchandise on English trading vessels, to be distributed in the different regions of Spain. The ever vigilant Inquisitors learned about this ruse, with the result that when an English vessel entered a Spanish port they went on board, others having been strictly prohibited to do so before them, and carried out a minute inspection of the cargo, seizing anything which could be used as heretical propaganda. The English sailors were only allowed to go ashore and move freely about the town, on condition that their behavior was in no way offensive to the Catholic religion. Every eventuality was provided for. If, for example, these sailors came upon a procession in which the Blessed Sacrament was being carried, or if they met a priest bringing Viaticum to a sick person, they were obliged to kneel or to go into a house—or, at all events, they were not to adopt a disrespectful or mocking attitude.

But what specially interests us is how and where in a country so ardently and jealously attached to the traditional faith, some centers could exist in which the doctrines of Luther and Calvin gained currency. The most important of these centers were at Valladolid and Seville. The first, which extended from Toro to Zamora, was principally inspired by Doctor Cazalla.

Another notorious propagandist was Roderigo de Valera who operated at Seville. The Inquisition imposed on him enforced residence in a monastery. These were contemporaries of Philip II.

Another adherent of the new doctrines was a Canon of Seville, Doctor John Gil, who later abjured his errors and was reconciled with the Church, or at least pretended to be so. After his death, a whole secret correspondence of his with the Protestants of Castile was discovered, and the Inquisitors had his body disinterred and burned.

Again in 1560, there was a certain Julianillo Hernandez whose propagandist activities in Seville, discovered by the Holy Office, led to the arrest of about eight hundred people. He was condemned to be burned alive at an *auto da fe* on December 22, 1560. Among the Andalusian Protestants of some eminence, there were Doctor Constantino, who provided a parallel to Doctor Cazalla in Castile, and Don John Ponce of Leon who ended his life by being put to death by strangulation in prison. A whole group of Lutheran adherents came into the hands of the Inquisition; some were burned alive, while others succeeded in escaping abroad, notably to London. Two Sevillan heretics, installed in London and assisted by the Queen, were Casiodoro and Cipriano de Valera who worked on a translation of the Bible into Spanish.

Among the Andalusian adherents of Protestantism, we even find some religious of the Convent of Saint Isidore of Seville. Warned of danger from the Inquisition; two of them succeeded in secretly escaping from the town, while the others were allowed by the Court of the Holy Office to do penance and to be reconciled.

All in all, perhaps the group of Castilian Protestants of Valladolid was more important than that of Seville. On May 21, 1559, Trinity Sunday, a great *auto da fe* took place in Valladolid against the adherents of Luther. Fourteen were handed over to the secular arm and burned, while many others were reconciled. The Lutherans of Valladolid assembled in the house of Dona Leonora de Vibero, widow of Peter Cazalla whose brother was the Doctor Cazalla already referred to. The most active of this numerous family was Doctor Augustine Cazalla, who was a priest and had been renowned as a preacher. Arrested by the Inquisition, he was condemned to the fire, but showed signs of genuine repentance before he died in the flames, exhorting those present to be warned by his example.

On October 2, 1559, in the reign of Philip II, an *auto da fe* took place in Valladolid at which the King himself presided, accompanied by the young Don Carlos and his sister Dona Juana. A great number of eminent people surrounded the King, among them the Duke of Parma, the Archbishop of Seville and the Constable of Castile. Among the guilty who mounted the platform were a gentleman of high lineage and a Dominican belonging to an aristocratic family, the de Pozas. The latter, after having been defrocked, was handed over to the secular arm on the accepted principle that noble birth increased the guilt of the accused. A certain number of religious and of followers of La Beata de Piedrahita (of whom we shall deal later) were condemned to life imprisonment during the same *auto*. On the same occasion, the remains of a religious posthumously convicted of heresy were ordered to be exhumed and burned.

These occurrences, and many others, which figure in the annals of the Spanish Inquisition, have been the subject of severe criticism by historians, and have become the basis of the legend of Spanish fanaticism. No doubt, the passage of centuries has not diminished the horror caused at the thought of those leaping flames, but it must be remembered that this sad spectacle was not an exclusively Spanish one. Furthermore, it cannot be denied that the vigilance and the extreme severity of the Holy Office in Spain, did preserve that country from the appalling bloodshed which, in the sixteenth and even the seventeenth centuries, accompanied the wars of religion caused by the Protestant Reformation, in France, in Germany, in England, and elsewhere. Even those who regard the maintenance of the purity of the Catholic faith as much less important than the practice of a certain tolerance, must admit this and take it into consideration. But this is a hindsight view; the cold cruelty of the Inquisition cannot be excused on these grounds.

Besides the relatively few adherents of Lutheranism and Calvinism, the Spanish Inquisition had to concern itself with the Enlightened, the *alumbrados,* who may be regarded as the original source of the Quietism of the Spanish priest, Molinos, which caused such violent controversies in the second half of the seventeenth century. The Enlightened of Spain were a sect of enthusiasts who claimed to behave in accordance with the "light" (hence the name) directly communicated to them by God. One of their earliest leaders was a laborer's daughter from Salamanca, known as La Beata de Piedrata, who in 1511 had been summoned before the Inquisitor as claiming to hold conversations with Christ and Our Lady. In the sixteenth century, we find three principal groups of the alumbrados—in Toledo and, later on, in Salamanca and Valladolid. These groups were generally under the immediate influence and direction of a woman. Do we not find a parallel in France, at a later date, in Madame Guyon? One of the most prominent "beata" was Francisca Hernandez who gathered around her, in Valladolid, a group of fervent disciples.

Between 1518 and 1527, the "alumbrados" finally came under suspicion. Alonso Manrique, Archbishop of Seville and Grand Inquisitor, published a decree against them, enumerating their errors and the social danger they represented, both on the religious and the moral plane. Much later, between 1570 and 1582, there was a group of the alumbrados in Lierena who, under the influence of their false mysticism, indulged in dangerous deviations of a sexual and psychic kind. One of them even went to the lengths of describing marriage as "a pig sty". There are certain analogies between these false mystics and the Cathari of Languedoc whom we discussed in an earlier chapter.

With Spanish Illuminism may be bracketed a number of cases of pseudo-ecstatics whom the Holy Office discovered, especially in convents of nuns. There were nuns who enjoyed the complete confidence even of the Kings of Spain, and who were nevertheless prosecuted by the Inquisitors as propagators of superstition. These cases are so frequent that they occurred up to the end of the eighteenth century—for instance, that of Dona

Teresa Dusmet, whose spiritual writings were condemned.

On several occasions, the Spanish Inquisition brought actions of far greater importance than the prosecution of more or less obscure "beatas", witches or alleged witches, or even hidden ahherents of the Protestant Reform. There was, for instance, the famous case of Bartolome de Carranza (1503-1576), Dominican theologian and a man of such eminence that from 1554 to 1557 he had resided in England as adviser to Philip II in the affair of his marriage to Mary I, and in the latter year was named by Philip as Archbishop of Toledo and Primate of Spain. From 1560, he was suspected by the Inquisition of having published works tainted with Erasmianism, and arrested the year after his consecration to be tried at Valladolid. The Archbishop of Valladolid refused to have anything to do with the matter, since he did not see eye to eye with the Grand Inquisitor, Fernando Valdes, Archbishop of Seville. Despite the fact that in 1563 the Council of Trent declared his work to be theologically sound, Carranza was imprisoned for nearly seventeen years.

The case had been referred to Rome, where it dragged on under the Pontificates of Pius IV, Pius V and Gregory XIII, and ended in 1576 when Carranza abjured seventeen propositions extracted from his writings. He was acquitted on April 14, but he was then confined to the Dominican Priory of the Minerva, where he died on May 2 of the same year, only eighteen days later.

In 1579, Antonio Perez, private secretary to Philip II, was accused of political crimes and of the assasina-

tion of John de Escobedo, friend and adviser of the
Governor of the Netherlands, Don Juan of Austria.
After many vicissitudes, he was accused of heresy by
the Inquisition and he fled to Bern. He was convicted
of contumacy and burned in effigy. Eventually, he
died in Paris. His sons showed tireless zeal in laboring
to secure the rehabilitation of his memory, and, after
long and painful efforts, succeeded in doing so, in
1615.

For a time, the Perez affair agitated public opinion
in Spain, and the same can be said of the case brought
(in the eighteenth century) against an illustrious Knight
of the Order of Calatrava, Don Jeronimo de Villa-
nueva, founder of a convent of the reformed Benedictine
nuns. A Benedictine—Francisco Garcia Calderon, al-
moner in Don Jeronimo's monastery—was also impli-
cated in the case. Extraordinary phenomena, of an
allegedly demoniac kind, having occurred in the convent, Don Jeronimo and the chaplain were subjected
to an interminable trial. King Philip himself took an
interest in the case. The Benedictine Monk was obliged
to pronounce a formula of abjuration at Toledo, and
was then condemned to spend the rest of his life in
a monastic cell at Valladolid, fasting three times a
week. Several of the nuns of the convent in question
(San Placido), received sentences of the same kind.
Don Jeronimo, energetically defended by the Procurator General of his Order, ended by making an appeal
to Rome, where the acts of his case were reexamined
and the sentence reversed.

Many cases of a similar kind are found in the
annals of the Holy Office, directed especially against
religious who combined phenomena of a more or less

adulterated mysticism with activities of a political kind. In these matters, extreme vigilance was used. We know that Philip IV was for long under the influence of a genuine mystic, the Blessed Maria d'Agreda; but, on the other hand, the influence of the priest, Molinos, the grand master of Quietism, was disastrous for certain people. There were cases in Murcia, in Oviedo, and in other places, where the Inquisition stepped in.

One comes upon curious cases as late as the eighteenth century. There was, for instance, that of a rich lord, Don Pablo de Olavida, who, after long journeys and residence abroad during which he had been an avid reader of Voltaire and the Encyclopaedists, was given a high post in Seville, and was finally arrested in 1776 by the Holy Office. He was tried and condemned to enforced residence in one or other of several places, notably in Murcia and Catalonia, under surveillance in Capuchin Friaries.

Sufficient has been said to show the "zeal" displayed by the Spanish Inquisition in its efforts to preserve in that country the purity of the Catholic faith. Against the fact that many were condemned to the flames, through the activities of the Holy Office, religious peace was assured to Spain but at a terrible price. There is, of course, an accusation levelled by so many writers that it must claim our attention. The shackles placed by the Inquisition on freedom of research and on the expression of opinions whose boldness could extend to formal heresy, proved harmful to Spanish culture and kept the country in a backward condition.

One point particularly relevant here is to establish to what extent the Inquisition was popular in Spain and upheld by the vast majority of the people. The various cases we have reviewed—"conversos", moriscos, adherents of Lutheranism and Calvinism, "alumbrados" —are very highly exceptional in relation to the whole population. Spaniards then considered, as the majority still do today, that their country was given a special mission by Providence to preserve the deposit of the Catholic faith in all its purity, and to kindle the torch of that faith in far off lands. For the false notion of tolerance as spread in France, especially during the eighteenth century, Spain substituted horror at the idea of the adulteration of that deposit of revealed truth confided to the Church by her Divine Founder.

This is something which is offensive to many in our day, even among Catholics. At least, one may enquire whether Spain's championship of orthodoxy resulted in a weakening of her culture and in relegation to the ranks of a backward country. Let us seek our answer from a writer who is liberal: "What is beyond denial or discussion is that the most flourishing epoch of our national life, as regards political predominance, military might, literature and the arts, coincides with that of the greatest Catholic fervor." Throughout his monumental work, the great critic and literary historian, Don Marcelino Menendez y Pelayo, loses no opportunity to emphasize this statement.

If there is one name which suffices in itself to proclaim the Spanish culture of the *siglo de oro* (the golden era), it is that of the great Cardinal Jimenez de Cisneros, Archbishop of Toledo and Primate of Spain. His generous protection of the Andalusian humanist, Nebriza, author of important works on the texts of Holy Scripture, and thereby under suspicion by the Grand Inquisitor, adequately shows the breadth of mind characteristic of this prince of the Church.

There were, of course, cases such as that of the Augustinian Friar, Luis of Leon, professor at Salamanca, imprisoned by the Inquisition for several years; and there was the whole business of the publication in Spain of the works of Erasmus, defended by some, attacked by others, and excessively suspected by the Holy Office. Such things did not hinder a healthy liberty of culture, however, and there were always qualified defenders to make the right cause triumph.

On account of the doctrines of Luther and Calvin concerning the Bible, the Spanish Inquisition was particularly sensitive about anything touching on Biblical studies, just as Rome had been in connection with Galileo. Hence it was that learned humanists and exegetes such as Luis of Leon and Martinez of Cantalapiedra, both professors at Salamanca, had long tussles with the Holy Office. But there again, although the Inquisition often showed great hesitancy and reluctance, it never deliberately transgressed against justice. Fortunately these men who were the ornaments of Spanish learning ended by being entirely cleared through definitive sentences pronounced by the Court of the Holy Office.

What we have briefly summarized concerning the Inquisition in Spain, applies equally to its activity in Spanish America. The Holy Office was instituted in Peru, in Mexico, and in all the principal centers of the Spanish possessions in America. We need not detail the activities of the Inquisitors sent from Spain to the New World, beyond noting that they received a formal order not to harass the recently converted "Indios", from whom the same acute sense of strict orthodoxy could not be expected as was demanded from the "old Christians".

Cases of bigamy, and even polygamy, were featured especially among the cases brought by the ecclesiastical judges in Mexico, Lima and elsewhere. In the course of the sixteenth and seventeenth centuries, there were several *autos da fe* in the capitals of Mexico and Peru, where the vast majority of the accused were reconciled.

The Inquisition in general, and the Spanish Inquisition in particular, will long continue to be the subject of heated discussion. The Inquisition was the child of its times, it reflected the temper and intolerance which our era would decry. The evils of the institution will hardly be forgotten: they should not be. But the Inquisition must be seen in its historical setting, it can only be judged in it... and the good it accomplished and the iniquities which it perpetrated must be weighed with detachment. The Inquisition is a fact of history, like Dachau and Katelyn: it is something which appalls modern man, it did not draw the same reaction in its centuries of operation, when religious tolerance and freedom of conscience were hardly seriously considered in any country or by any segment of society. It is something we might like to explain or explain away; its barbarities should be remembered—for the faith cannot and should not be defended by methods and means which distort the very meaning of faith and which show a basic disrespect for the human person.